SPIRITED

SPIRITED

Connect to the Guides
All Around You

Rebecca Rosen

with Samantha Rose

Foreword by James Van Praagh

HARPER

An Imprint of HarperCollinsPublishers
www.harpercollins.com

Designed by Ellen Cipriano
ISBN 978-0-06-176624-4

This book is dedicated to my grandmother, Ruth "Babe" Perelman, and my beloved father, Shelly Perelman.

I'm eternally grateful for your guiding light, unconditional love, and inspiration along my journey.

CONTENTS

FOREWORD

Each of us is a unique, multilayered amalgam of wiring specifically designed for our particular souls. We all come to this planet as spiritual beings destined to experience a variety of challenges and situations in order to grow and evolve spiritually.

When we take the time to enter into a relationship with our inner selves and become aware or in tune with our spiritual heritage, we embark upon a special journey. This journey is a process of peeling away layers of conditioning, self-doubt, and self-imposed rules of control. By opening up to our "inner guidance system," we experience insight and "knowingness," which we may have never experienced before. Based on our natural heritage as the divine light of God, every one of us possesses intuition—defined as the language of the soul. Once you develop this part of yourself, you can utilize this natural tuning fork and employ it in your everyday life.

Possessing intuition is having an absolute trust in yourself. It is the only way to fulfill your highest aspirations and desires. Everyone wants a life of happiness, health, and prosperity, but never seems to know the road to take for this to be realized. When you become aware of your intuition, you are delving inside and beginning to know yourself and becoming aware of your own personal rhythm. On this journey you must be willing to look at yourself objectively and clear away any judgments imposed on you by family, friends, or even society. I have found in many of my workshops that in order for people to really go deep within and discover their intuitive self, they will inevitably have to go through old tapes—old patterns and programming they received earlier in life. It is very much like cleaning out your garage, going through boxes of stuff that you no longer need, because you are a different person. When you open up, you also must face certain emotions that you may have buried deep down and long ago. You cannot hear the inner voice clearly if there are emotional obstructions or fears in the way.

When you learn to access and follow this part of you, you gain control of your life and begin to understand your soul's inner promptings, which will lead you to the right choices and the life you were meant to live. Soon, you find that your life will take you to places and through situations you never thought possible but inevitably knew were necessary.

This book is one woman's journey of self-discovery. When you read through it, you will see how difficult it was for her to acknowledge or accept that she had a high degree of intuition, let alone to listen to it. But she followed her instincts and used it as an opportunity to discover her true self. Now she utilizes that part of herself to serve humankind. With this book you too have been given an incredible opportunity to step inside your own distinct sense of knowing. This might seem strange or weird at first, since you may not be used to utilizing this part of your being. But that is all part of the exciting journey of discovering yourself.

One of the most endearing parts of this book to me (I am sure it will be to you, too) is the candor with which Rebecca describes the psychic world and her very own abilities. She takes what's often seen as a strange and elusive subject and turns it into something that is relatable to everyone in this tangible and physical world.

Whenever the word *psychic* is used, many cannot help but conjure up images of gypsies in storefronts throwing down tarot cards and gazing into crystal balls. Although that type of individual does exist, this is not what Rebecca and I refer to in our work. We are talking about your sixth sense, the same sense you used when you were a baby. Some also refer to it as instinct. This is inherent in each one of us. As a matter of fact, you use your intuition every day without even thinking about it. For instance, whenever the phone rings you probably attempt to guess who is calling you. Or when you stand in front of a row of elevators, you intuitively wonder which elevator door will open first. We use intuition as a way to connect with our divine self. One does not necessarily need to be religious or spiritual or even to pray. Our connection with our intuitive self is ever present and always a part of ourselves.

As the great psychologist John Lilly once said, your only limits are your beliefs. It is true. Knowledge is power and being aware of your intuitive self is your key to unlocking the gifts of your soul. Ever since I became aware of my intuitive self and developed it, I began to see the world around me with a new and keen perspective, and my values, ideals, and awareness took on a higher meaning.

This book offers you the same chance to engage, question, and explore yourself through the eyes of a woman who has made the courageous journey to step outside her comfort zone and truly find the meaning of life. I wish the same for you and that the path ahead will forever change you, inspiring you to always reach for what you cannot see, beyond the physical self.

James Van Praagh

Introduction

Hi. Let me introduce myself. My name is Rebecca Rosen. I'm in my thirties, happily married, a working mother, and a Denver suburbanite. I struggle with my share of good and bad days and how to juggle my career with the needs of my family. *Sound familiar?* I'm a regular gal like many of you. There's just *one* little twist: I'm a professional psychic medium. I communicate with spirits on a regular basis—*you know*, dead people who linger around to provide advice and offer relief to the living. Now, don't roll your eyes—I'm not your stereotypical woo-woo. No flowing robes, no lingering scent of patchouli. I look and talk just like many of my "normal" clients. In fact, you may have seen me explaining my uncommon job on TV or read about me in your local paper and thought, *She doesn't look too out-there.*

Most of the time, clients seek me out because they can't get past the death of a loved one and their grief is dragging down their spirit and getting in the way of their everyday lives. I can sympathize with this kind of debilitating pain because I, too, lost someone very near and dear to me not long ago and it wrecked me in a big way. It seemed like I wandered around for months and months asking the same question, *Why? Why? Why? Why did this have to happen?*

For nearly ten years now, clients have come to me hoping that I will connect them with a cherished loved one who has passed on, or at least provide them with the comfort that someone they love is no longer in pain. As a medium, it's been my honor to provide solace and relief for thousands of grieving people. But a few years ago, I started to notice a shift in the familiar needs and requests of my clients. In addition to people who were grieving the loss of a loved one, others came to see me: those who were simply hungry for spiritual truth and a deeper under-standing of why they felt lost and stuck in their lives. Initially I kidded with them, "Well, you know I'm not a *therapist*, but let me take a look and see what your loved ones have to say." Well, the joke was finally on me because after countless readings where I connected clients with Spirit, an undeniable pattern started taking shape that became the inspi-ration for this book.

After receiving validations, or proof, that their loved ones were at peace and still with them on some level, clients were also getting insights about how to get unstuck and move on with their lives. That's right—in addition to offering closure around their deaths, spirits started coming through to help the living with their very down-to-Earth, daily prob-lems! I remember thinking, *So, the dead are the new self-help experts now?!*

I'll never forget one of the first times this happened, early on in my career. I was lying in *savasana* in yoga class one day, when I started to hear "Papa Maurie" over and over again in my head. *I don't know a Papa Maurie—not even a Maurie*, I thought. But the name continued to come up and then an image of my friend Stacy flashed in my mind. In this picture, she was breaking up with her boyfriend of many years. I heard this Papa Maurie character saying, "Tell her to let him go. It's the right thing."

The information made no sense to me at the time. Stacy seemed perfectly happy in her relationship, and again—*Who was Papa Maurie?* I put the vision out of my mind until the following night when I met Stacy for dinner. After we sat down at our favorite sushi restaurant

I asked her how she was doing and she immediately burst into tears. She told me that she and her boyfriend had just decided to call it quits. (As in, the night before when I was sitting in yoga class!) *That's really weird,* I thought to myself. I sat on this for a minute and then I asked, "Stacy, by any chance do you know a Papa Maurie who passed?" (At this point, Stacy was used to my medium-speak.) "Are you serious?" she asked. "Papa Maurie was my grandfather!"

Once I told her about the voice and vision, she felt better about her decision to end it with her boyfriend, although she was a little weirded out by the notion that her dead grandpa was keeping a watch on her love life and offering her relationship advice!

Months later, Stacy and her boyfriend got back together and despite her own doubts and concerns, they took it to the next level: They got engaged. I had my own reservations about her decision, but kept my opinions to myself. It was her life and not for me to interfere. When she came to me and asked if I'd try to connect her with her grandfather, I obliged, and again, Papa Maurie came through and told her that Jason was not "the one" and not to marry him. It was a very awkward moment for us. She was a good friend and I was giving her information she really didn't want to hear. Stacy decided to ignore her Papa's advice and married Jason soon afterward. We never spoke of the reading again until six years later when Stacy and Jason, then with a three-year-old and a newborn, announced they were getting divorced. She came to me with regret, saying that she'd never forgotten the advice from her Papa. She finally understood that he was only trying to save her years of heartache and pain. He'd been right after all: Jason was not the one.

ACTING AS A MEDIUM, or middle gal, between Spirit and clients, I've helped thousands of people just like you wake up to the reality of their lives and name the thing that's standing in their way. And no, it's not always a guy! In our sessions, clients and I are constantly tackling:

grief

relationship problems

financial woes

low self-esteem

depression

intimacy fears

substance abuse

anger

control issues

weight problems

While this was not the career I originally intended for myself (I was pursuing an advertising degree when the spirits started squawking), I feel so lucky to have found a calling where I'm able to help people get to the bottom of their discontent and resolve the personal challenge that's keeping them from becoming the person they've always wanted to be.

In the pages that follow, you'll see that *Spirited* is grounded in real life stories and real people. Whenever clients thank me for providing them with clarity, hope, and relief when they needed it most, I always think, *This is why I do this crazy work.* But I want to let you in on a little secret: *You actually don't need me, or any other psychic, to resolve any of the issues I've just described.* You can learn to connect with your inner intelligence and get clear all on your own. Not by becoming a psychic medium, but by just being you. Truly, the only difference between you and me is that I've mastered a skill that you haven't developed yet—a skill that could help you identify where you're stuck and get you back on track to leading a purposeful and fulfilled life. By developing your own intuitive power, you will learn to trust and depend on your knowing, as well as recognize and interpret spirit energy—a support system available to you at any time.

Spirited is all about *you* learning to find the answers within and around yourself. By the time you finish this book, my hope is that you'll be able to say, "Thanks, Rebecca. No offense, but I don't need you anymore. I'll take it from here."

Maybe you're thinking, *I don't know—that sounds kind of nutty*, and I admit, when I first started developing my intuition and connection to Spirit, I had my share of skepticism, too. The idea of communicating with people who were no longer living seemed, well, *creepy*, and this is a popular and very common misconception. The truth is spirits don't mean us harm or want to freak us out. Quite the opposite, actually. Spirits constantly ask me to relay the same, simple message to their living loved ones—*Stop making the mistakes I did and start living already!* In most every case, spirits show up with no agenda other than to help us move past the thing that's in our way: sadness, guilt, an unhappy relationship, a bad job, negative body image, crippling credit card debt— everyday stuff. More than anything, they want us to remember the whole purpose of life: to live truly and freely in the present and enjoy every minute of our time here.

The idea that spirits are available to help us with such worldly concerns will take some time getting used to, which is why I'm going to walk you through the process step by step until you have the courage to go out on your own. Many of us, and women particularly, tend to discount our intuitive power and spiritual awareness. Why? Well, that's a topic for a whole other book, but in a nutshell, we're quick to second-guess ourselves. This is unfortunate because each one of us has the ability to tap into everyday guidance. Yes, even *you*. And my guess is that you picked up this book because you already *know* that—you're just not sure where to start tappin'. Well, that's where I come in. I'm going to hold your hand and show you the way.

Let's get started!

1

＊

Is This Woman for Real?

While many books on the afterlife are written to draw readers to the authors' private practices, my goal is to set you free of psychics and mediums altogether, by providing you with the tools to empower yourself and identify the root of your discontent all on your own. (By the way, this is not going to make me very popular with some of my peers!) I like to say that my program is "self-help," but with a lot more than just your "self" to help you through. In addition to learning how to tap into your intuitive power, you will learn to access the wisdom of those who are no longer living but who have a valuable perspective to share.

If you've never bought a book like this before or sought the advice of a psychic medium, you may be more accustomed to conventional approaches to resolving issues. In fact, I've had people ask me pointed questions like, "Rebecca, what's wrong with traditional therapy—you know, like where you sit on a couch across from someone with a psych background and who's *living*?" My answer is: nothing. A therapist can absolutely help you uncover the thing that's holding you back. But why not weed out a year's worth of sessions and get to the heart of the matter right now, by going *inside yourself* to get the guidance you need? You do know that you have all the answers within you, right? Granted, once you identify any pain that's hiding below the surface, you very well may want to talk to a therapist to help you process the information you've been given. At the end of every reading I do, I'm always sure to remind my clients that the insights I provide are merely the start of the healing process. "I've just lifted the veil," I say. "I haven't fixed anything. The rest is up to you."

BUT LET'S BACK UP. Right now you're probably at the point where you're thinking, *I know something's off with my life and I could be happier, but how can I start to heal if I don't even know what my problem is?* Good question. Many of us have pain, regrets, and disappointments buried so far deep down inside ourselves, we have no idea they're there or how they're manifesting in our everyday lives. My goal is to show you how to peel back the layers, dig into your past, and become conscious of what's keeping you stuck. This can be an uncomfortable process. You've buried hurts because—no mystery here—*they hurt!* Uncovering the heart of your discontent can be scary, lonely work, so that's where the gentle presence of Spirit comes in to remind you that you're not alone. (In fact, start repeating to yourself in the shower, in the car, or on the train into work—*I'm not alone, I'm not alone, I'm not alone!*) Think of the spirit energy surrounding you as your own cheerleading squad, keeping you company and supporting you along the way.

Now, that doesn't mean Spirit is going to do all the work for you. As I said, changing the direction of your life starts with you and it's a process that requires your strong and lasting commitment. No one gets toned arms overnight and it's the same with developing your intuitive and spiritual muscle. But, like my yoga instructor likes to say, "Stand tall and believe in your extraordinary strength. You will be amazed at what you can do!" And she's right—when you start to believe in yourself, you will be guided the rest of the way.

HOW TO USE THIS BOOK

There are a few different ways you can use this book and I urge you to choose the one that works best for YOU. After all, I developed this program so that you can do your own work, so take it at your own comfortable pace. It's kind of a no-brainer, but sometimes we forget that there is no right or wrong way of going about our own self-discovery.

> Option One: Read it straight through, skim over the heavy lifting exercises, and go back to do the big work once you've digested the basic concepts of the book.
>
> Option Two: Take it slow, pause to do the exercises, and sit with whatever you dig up before you move on to the next section.
>
> Option Three: Take it even slower! Some of these concepts might sound really weird to you the first time around. You might find yourself saying, *Hold on! I don't get it,* so I'll stop and answer some of the more head-scratching ideas as we go along. Still, there may be some sections (or entire chapters) that you'll want to reread once, twice, three times before moving forward. No problem. Again, take your time.

Okay, before we get started on *you* and personalizing a program to accommodate your lifestyle, I want to share some personal history with you because admit it—you're wondering, *Is this woman for real?* How does a seemingly normal chick become a psychic who talks to the dead?

Well, not only do I live like many of you, there's another thing we might share in common. Ten years ago, I was in a very dark place and I had no idea how to pull myself out of it.

MY PERSONAL DAMAGE

We've all had those mornings: You wake up and realize *this is not where I want my life to be* and *this is not who I REALLY am.* At those moments you remind yourself: *I've tried everything from retail therapy to couples counseling and the latest fad diet, and nothing's working. I'm not happy. I'm struggling. And I don't know why.*

Those mornings aren't any fun, are they?

On the other hand, the times when you find yourself, well, talking to yourself are also noteworthy because that's when you've allowed yourself—if only for ten seconds—to sneak a peek at what's really going on. That's clarity, which is just another way to say *understanding.* And getting clear is the first step to going from "I suck" to "I get it!"

Being able to truly see our lives is everyday magic—it's what happens when we are tuned into our intuition. People in my line of work call intuition a connection to Source, God, the Universe. Sometimes our intuitive voice can be superbly annoying—*Um, thanks, but I don't need to be reminded that my life is off-track*—but I'm here to tell you that when intuition whispers in your ear, you want to listen up. That voice can transform your life. It did mine.

Hold On! I Don't Get It: What is intuition, exactly?

Here's the Deal: Intuition goes by many names and expressions—Our higher self. Sixth sense. Inspired thought. Gut feeling. Clear knowing. That *Aha!* moment.

What This Means for You: When we are tuned into our intuition, the veil is lifted and the answers become clear. Most of us, sad to say, are out of touch with our intuition. We've learned to ignore, mistrust, and second-guess it and then we wonder why we feel so disconnected from ourselves, as if we're drifting around in a state of merely existing. Once we recognize and reconnect with our intuitive power, we start making better decisions and choices for our lives.

OKAY, NOW BACK TO my story. Ten years ago, I left my safe hometown of Omaha, Nebraska, for what so many high school graduates dream of: freedom and an exciting college experience. I entered the University of Florida, joined a great sorority, quickly made friends, had plenty of dates, and was at the top of my class. My life was the perfect picture of *on track*. But two thousand miles back home, the wheels had fallen off the train. My dad, who was a loving father, was withdrawn in every other area of his life. He'd been unhappy and introverted for years and when, within weeks of me starting school, Mom called with "bad news," I thought Dad had probably sunk back into one of his dark stages. The news was much worse—he'd attempted suicide. Thankfully, she and my brother were able to convince him to check into a psychiatric hospital, where doctors diagnosed him with manic depression and explained that he'd been chemically imbalanced for years. After eight days of rest and recovery and a prescribed diet of antidepressant medication, my father was back home safe and regaining strength, but my parents' marriage, which I knew wasn't perfect, but I believed was solid and enduring, was crumbling under the stress. I was shocked and devastated. My childhood sense of security suddenly felt like a big fat lie, and because I was so far from home and removed from the situation, I couldn't help feeling alone, scared, and angry that I hadn't somehow been there to stop it.

My mom urged me to stay put until the end of the school year. She would take care of Dad, she promised, and convinced me that I didn't need to worry. *Yeah, right.* Little did I know this episode was just the calm before a devastating storm.

When I returned home for the summer, although my father was

healthy and stable again, I watched my family fall apart. My feelings were complicated and painful, and, honestly, I couldn't wait to get back to school and escape the uncomfortable sadness of it all.

When I went back to school in the fall, I moved off campus and into an apartment with three roommates. I tried to forget about my home life by distracting myself with sorority events and my new classes, but within a couple of months, I slipped into depression. My grades started to suffer, I withdrew from everyone around me, and I found a destructive habit to numb my pain. I began eating—in my sleep. As in, getting up in the middle of the night and unconsciously consuming the contents of my fridge. Talk about a nightmare.

The "Night Prowler," what I named my new self-sabotaging personality, started making regular appearances every night of the week. I'd sleepwalk into the kitchen and stuff my mouth full of sweet and salty comfort foods—anything I could get my hands on. I'd wake up in the dark, not knowing how long I'd been there or how much I'd eaten. I'd return to bed feeling confused, scared, and totally out of control. I felt like a prisoner to myself and I spent countless nights crying myself back to sleep.

For six long months, this abusive cycle of binging continued. I told no one about the Night Prowler. I was so ashamed. Day after day, I would vow *I am NOT going to wake up!* But, night after night, I unconsciously chose otherwise. I repeated the same destructive habit like clockwork and every morning I'd wake up, full of self-loathing, berating myself over another night of eating.

During the day, I was like a zombie, living off cappuccinos and starving myself in an attempt to make up for the calories consumed at night. Then, after gaining nearly forty pounds, I had a major breakdown. For the first time since the Night Prowler appeared, I went home to Omaha and revealed my shameful secret to Mom and Dad. It was such a relief to finally reach out for help. After months of hiding the truth, I was emotionally exhausted and physically depleted. Despite their eroding marriage, my parents were selfless in their support and care. They found me a good therapist who helped me understand that I was using food like a drug just like my mother had. Mom struggled with an eating disorder for many years while I was growing up, and I watched and learned how to "stuff" feelings down with food. (We'll get into this in later chapters, but I strongly believe we all have a "drug of choice," and for me, it's food. For others, it might be drugs, alcohol, compulsive shopping, or controlling behavior. Instead of using your "drug" to numb your feelings and ignore the truth about your life, I will help you find the courage to WAKE UP and begin listening to the wisdom of your intuitive voice. It is this voice—*your voice*—that will tell you what you need to do to face and heal your pain.)

My therapist put me on antidepressant medication and, for the first time in months, I felt hopeful that I would snap out of my funk, stop binging, and return to a normal life. But I quickly learned that the medication was not enough—as soon as I returned to school, the Night Prowler returned. I was desperate—*What the hell is going on here? Why am I doing this? Why can't I stop?* You might be asking the same questions about your situation.

On the brink of giving up and slipping into a dangerous place, I did the only thing I knew left to do. One night, after my roommates went to bed, I closed my door, got down on my hands and knees, and began to pray. Quite literally, my prayers sounded like, *Help me, help me, help me. Is there anyone who can help me?* And, as I was soon to find out, my cries were heard. My grandmother Babe—my father's mother, who died when I was a little girl—answered the call.

ADVICE FROM BABE

I've always written in a journal as a way to gain clarity and express myself. Maybe you're someone who does this, too? I think journaling is a great way to make sense of the jumbled thoughts that spin around in our heads, keeping us confused and afraid. A day or so after my desperate cry for help, I sat down with my journal in a neighborhood bookstore and wrote out my shameful confession, just as I had done many times before. As always, I hoped that I would gain some new insight about how to overcome my struggles.

On this particular afternoon, as soon as I began to write, I noticed a resistance in the flow of my words that I hadn't felt before and I stopped. It was like I could hear a voice in my head talking over my own thoughts. Goose bumps traveled up and down my arms. When I resumed writing, I felt a strong tug on my hand. My pen then proceeded to drag in a scribble-like way. Within minutes, a free flow of information was flying across page after page, conveying messages from a woman who identified herself as—get this—my dead grandmother Babe. Thoughts soon started coming into my mind faster than I could get them down on paper, and they weren't words or a vernacular I would normally use. *Okay,* I thought, *something weird is going on here because this is definitely not me!* I'm certain that if this were to happen to you, you'd assume you had totally lost it, which is exactly how I felt. But, at the same time, I was so desperate for help that I was willing to suspend my disbelief and see what happened next. (I later discovered that I was "automatic writing," a psychic practice used by many mediums to convey messages from Spirit. A spirit focuses energy to "write" through your hand.) For the next hour, Babe told me why she had come through: *I've heard your cries at night and I don't want you to suffer the same way I did.*

My grandmother Babe had had a hard life. She suffered from mental illness brought on by postpartum depression. Unfortunately, the methods for treating depression in the early 1960s were cruel and often ineffective. My grandmother was given tranquilizers and shock therapy treatments for many years. These methods did not alleviate her sadness or pain; they left an even darker hole in her heart that she was never able to fill. Sadly, she eventually took her own life.

In the bookstore that day, Babe said, *Don't be afraid. I am here to free you from pain.* She expressed her desire for me to make different and better choices than she did. And by helping me out of my depression, she could also heal her own soul, kind of like a psychic win-win, balancing out her—let's call it—negative mojo. You see, by taking her own life, Babe didn't make a clean or easy getaway—she just carried the wounds she had into the afterlife.

Hold On! I Don't Get It: Are you saying that you take all your messed-up stuff with you after you die?

Here's the Deal: Your damage doesn't just go away—it follows you until you face it, deal with it, and release it.

What This Means for You: After working with Spirit over the years, I am convinced that how we conduct ourselves in this life follows us into the afterlife. In other words, we may eventually leave our bodies, but we take our baggage with us.

What I hear from spirits day in and day out are their regrets about poor choices and bad decisions they made in life. Some mention how careless and reckless they were with the people they loved. Many wish they'd spent less time working and more time with their children. They feel remorse over their personal failures like alcoholism and drug addiction, finally realizing the impact their actions had on the safety and happiness of their families. They often say they shouldn't have taken their health for granted. They lament missed opportunities and wish they'd lived outside their comfort zone with more risks. The list goes on and on.

In nearly every reading I do, Spirit comes through to make amends for their regrettable actions, or inactions, in life and to offer guidance for the living. They either want their loved ones to do what they *didn't* do, or not do what they *did*. But I'm getting ahead of myself. Let's get back to Grandma Babe before we delve into a heavy discussion about "life after death."

Babe stressed that for me to work out *my* damage and heal, I had to begin loving myself unconditionally. She was clear that my destructive habit would continue until I did this hard work, but she was here to help since I'd asked for it. Crazy, right?

Like anyone would be, I was skeptical that my dead grandmother was truly "talking" to me, and Babe sensed my doubt that first day. She instructed me to call my father for proof. *Ask him*, she said, *about the white sheets.* White sheets? I had no idea what this meant, but I immediately left the bookstore and called my dad to relay the message anyway. He was speechless for a beat, and then he let out an astounded, "Oh my God!" He proceeded to confirm what Babe said with this story:

The day that my grandmother took her life, my grandfather came home from work and found the house uncharacteristically quiet. His wife was nowhere to be found and when he discovered the basement door ajar, he suddenly feared the worst. He didn't have the courage to walk down to the basement, so he called my father and asked him to come over to either confirm or deny his foreboding feeling. My father had been my grandmother's emotional caretaker for years, so it made sense that he would be the one to handle a potential crisis. As soon as my father arrived and took his first step down the basement stairs, he could smell the gunpowder. Once he reached the bottom step, he instinctively turned toward the laundry room, where he found his sixty-seven-year-old mother in a heap on bloodstained white sheets. She'd shot herself in the mouth. Known for her spotless home, she'd laid sheets out on the floor before pulling the trigger to make the clean up easy. My father never told anyone about his mother's tidiness that fateful day. That is, until the afternoon I called him from the bookstore and said very pointedly, "Grandma wants you to tell me about the white sheets."

I was shocked by the validation and totally overwhelmed. *So, it was true? I'd just communicated with Grandma Babe!* That first day of auto-

A Note on Skepticism

It's perfectly normal for you to have a big, healthy dose of this. Ninety percent of the world lives in a mind existence (i.e., *I won't believe it until I see it!*), so believing and trusting in something that isn't tangible is hard for many of us to do. In the following chapters, I will show you how to read the signs and "see" for yourself.

matic writing was a major turning point for me and the beginning of my understanding that spirits, when called, will intervene in our healing process. Because I wasn't ready to face the root of my pain alone, Grandma Babe, who'd struggled similarly in life, came through to hold my hand as I looked in the mirror. This is an important point. Spirits help us connect with our intuitive power, where clear knowing resides. They don't provide the answers; rather, they serve to illuminate the truth that is within us all the time.

So, what was at the root of my emotional eating? I grew up with a father who believed a person was weak for showing emotion, which had everything to do with his own mother's emotional instability and the painful hold it had on him growing up. (I'll touch on this a little later, but my father had a tremendous amount of unresolved grief and guilt tied to his mother's death.) As a kid, he often scolded me for pouting and being "too sensitive." My dad would rather people pretend to be happy than reveal their discontent or pain. Because like many women, I am a people pleaser (who also adored her father), I perfected the "everything's fine" perma-grin by early adulthood. And since it wasn't safe to express emotions growing up, I learned how to stuff them down—just like my mother and her self-destructive relationship with food. Are you starting to recognize the dysfunctional family pattern here? Jeez—what a mess!

BACK TO MY SOPHOMORE year in college. I was devastated by my father's suicide attempt and my parents' impending divorce, but I was house-trained to suppress negative emotions, and that's exactly what I did. As time went on and with no release for how sad and heartbroken I felt inside, my soul began shaking me awake in the middle of the night—*Wake up! Rebecca, wake up!* But instead of listening to clarity whispering in my ear, I was literally stuffing the pain back down because I was too scared to let it come to the surface. Why? Because I didn't want to disappoint my father by saying how I really felt. God forbid I upset anyone! I'd gotten in the unhealthy habit of putting a higher value on pleasing, or placating, others than honoring my own needs. Well, my soul had had it! My soul cried out—*SPEAK!* And when I finally did, I cried out . . . *I'M SCARED. I'M HEARTBROKEN. I'M ANGRY. I'M HURT! I blame myself for not being able to keep my family together. I have failed those I love. AND I CAN'T KEEP QUIET ANYMORE!*

I know now how flawed that thinking was and that I was punishing myself unfairly. Of course it wasn't my responsibility to keep my parents together, nor could I have stopped my father's suicide attempt. But that's what initially came to the surface when I broke the silence and dis-lodged the truth. Once I gave myself permission to feel freely, I began to see more clearly. That's what I mean when I say "lifting the veil." It's like seeing your life for the first time in a long while.

When we're feeling lost, defeated, or alone, it's hard to believe that the answers are inside us, and that's often because we've cut ourselves off from our inner knowing. Given enough time, this state of disconnection can lead to depression and self-abusive behavior. Clearly, I'm evidence of that! When we hit bottom, we have an important choice to make—we can either recognize our self-abusive behavior as a wake-up call and do the necessary work to reconnect and heal, or we can choose to continue down the same broken road. Door number one sounds a whole lot better, doesn't it? But so many of us choose door number two. Why is this? Because we aren't ready, or don't know how to dig in and do the work. Many of us resist change (you know who you are), and the rest of us are simply afraid to confront the block in our path—*It's too big. It's too scary. I'm not strong enough to move it!*

My grandma came through when she did because, well, it was pretty obvious that I needed a hand. Babe could see that I'd simply had enough self-abuse and I was ready to do whatever it took to resolve it. She stepped in to illuminate my way.

After that pivotal afternoon in the bookstore, I continued to use automatic writing to connect with my grandmother. She helped me look at the layers of my pain and decide what I needed to do in order to heal on all levels: exercise and yoga to shed my extra weight, less caffeine and sugar to ease my anxiety and aid in better sleep, daily journaling to release all my feelings, prayer to invite in spirit energy, meditation to strengthen a connection to my intuitive voice, and most important, working on building up my self-esteem and inner knowing rather than looking outside of myself for answers and approval. I had my work cut out for me, but I was so eager to free myself from my self-destructive patterns, once I realized what those were, I was willing to do whatever it took.

My work with Babe continued for two years and I'll be honest— it wasn't easy, but eventually the Night Prowler disappeared. I lost the bulk of my weight, my depression faded away, and I felt healthy and happy again.

Toward the end of my senior year in college, Babe came through during my journaling and told me her work with me was done. It was time, she said, for us to go our separate ways. (It felt like my grandma was breaking up with me.) I was healthy, she said, and it was my responsibility now to help others who were struggling and needed relief.

Although my initial reaction was, *No way—I don't want to become that lady with jangling bracelets and a crystal ball.*

THE WEIRDNESS FACTOR

You see, even after all my work with Babe, I still had my hesitations. I knew I had some kind of "gift," but it was hard to get past the weirdness factor. Seriously, introductions at dinner parties were going to be awkward—"Hi, I'm Rebecca, your friendly neighborhood psychic medium." I admit, I thought about bagging the whole idea. But I didn't. Why? Well, because my dark Night Prowler episodes were finally behind me and I had Babe and my psychic abilities to thank for it. It wouldn't be fair to ignore my ability to connect with Spirit if it could help other people, right? Still, I was very nervous to take my act on the road and test it out on *perfect strangers.* The thought made me feel as hesitant as when I'd first started the whole "talking to the dead" business.

It wasn't until a year after graduating that I was brave enough to begin playing around with automatic writing and the Ouija board (also known as a spirit or talking board) with friends. Finally, in front of an audience, I connected with spirits, completely unknown to me, who offered validations that convinced all of us that I was tapping into something beyond my own awareness. Still, I sensed that it was too threatening or "out there" for my friends to wrap their college-educated minds around. They basically dismissed it as a weird party game and didn't take it seriously.

But I did take it seriously. I began a habit of pulling the board out late at night and playing with it in secret (that way, I didn't run the risk of being labeled "creepy séance girl"). I'd pray for Spirit to come through and connect with me. Well, one night, the planchette started to slowly move around the board, spelling out, "Hello, Rebecca. I am your angel." *Okay,* I thought, *maybe I* am *creepy séance girl!* My heart started to race as the planchette continued to move across the board in a furious race for several minutes until it abruptly stopped. I wasn't quite sure what had just happened, but I felt comforted by the idea that an angel was keeping me company. *Angels were good, right?* I put the board away and called it a night.

The following evening, I again locked myself in my room and pulled the board out. I lit a large candle on a stand in the corner of the room and sat on my bed with the board in my lap. I mentally said a prayer to invite in the "Angel." It took a few minutes before I felt any movement, and then the energy slowly came in. Angel lady told me she was my guardian angel, Maya. Her energy felt very loving and I got the sense that she was wise and I could trust her. Maya said she was hanging out with Grandma Babe to help me with my depression. *Angelic back up? Are you joking?* Like my roommates, I started to wonder if this was really happening and if I wasn't just making the whole thing up in my crazy head. And then, as if Maya heard my doubtful thoughts, she spelled out, "Candle dripping, candle dripping." I was totally confused by this until I heard a soft dripping sound behind me. I quickly turned around and saw that the candle I'd lit was dripping wax onto my floor! I jumped up off the bed and blew it out. I was shocked. It was the first time I really felt as if there was another presence in the room with me—that I was not alone. (I imagine this would make a lot of you feel uneasy, but I wasn't scared. I sensed that Maya was a gentle and caring presence. Not anything dark or to be feared.)

Over the next several months, I continued to test my connection with Spirit and when summer rolled around again, I found myself back home spending time with my dad and his business partner Seth. Dad had done a total 180 since his suicide attempt. He was actually communicative and open. He liked to talk about *feelings*. He explained that the day he left his hospital room, he felt like he was having an out-of-body experience. When he turned around to take one last look at his hospital bed, he saw "Shel" being left behind to die and a new man, "Shelly," emerging. He was convinced that he had shed his unhappy "shell" and he was now a new and changed man. And truly, he *was* a different person: He was softer, kinder, and hungry for spiritual truth. In fact, soon after I became aware of my intuitive gift, Dad became my greatest supporter. He had absolute faith and belief in me and encouraged me to embrace my calling to do "God's work." Quite a turnaround from his earlier criticism of my sensitivity!

One afternoon with Dad and Seth that summer, I was playing around with automatic writing when a spirit named "Larry" came through. I couldn't think of anyone that Dad or I knew by that name, so I asked Seth, "Do you know anyone named Larry?" He was dumbfounded.

"That's my father," he said. "He's been dead a long time."

"Well," I said, "he's telling me that he's very sorry about his sudden death and how it tore the family apart. He also wants me to mention the briefcase?"

Seth stared at me with tears in his eyes. He then confided in me that his father had died when Seth was just a teenager. The only thing that he still had of his father's was his briefcase.

After that day, I couldn't deny that I was making very real and solid connections with Spirit, not only for myself, but to help others. I started doing readings with friends of friends—without the Ouija board—and after a half dozen successful readings, I realized that my gift was not about me. If my ability was as accurate and as healing as people were telling me it was, I knew I had to share it in a big way. I knew it was time to head out into the real world.

The first public readings I did were in the back of a local coffee shop. I sat with clients on a couch with a legal pad and I'd ask Spirit to speak to me. I was still using automatic writing to relay messages. Because I was a bit nervous at first, worried that I wouldn't always be able to make connections for *real* people, these initial readings were not as clear as they could have been. Still, it didn't take long for me to recognize that however unclear, I was having a powerful effect on others.

✦ TESTIMONIALS

Dear Rebecca,

I have been grieving my father for close to a year now. The reading that we had has made such an impact on me that I honestly don't know how to explain it to you. I had never done anything like this before and was always a little skeptical, although it was something that I always wanted to believe. And there is no doubt in my mind now. My father spoke to me through you. It has given me new breath. I know he is with me and I know he will always be with me. I have complete faith in that. Thank you for that. It is truly a gift and I am grateful that I was able to find you and have you share it with me.

Sincerely,

Elizabeth from Dania, Florida

Hi Rebecca,

I just wanted to thank you again for sharing your time and amazing gift with me yesterday. I can't even explain how it has affected me. I have been living with so much confusion and doubt recently, and so many of the things you said and validations you offered cleared up so much of that; it's as if a huge weight has been lifted from my shoulders.

Respectfully,

Karrie from Hesperia, California

In those early café days when I was establishing my credibility in the community, many people came in guarded and somewhat disbelieving. When I noticed this resistance, I would acknowledge it by saying, "I'm not here to make you a believer. Let the messages speak for themselves and then believe if you want to." Nine out of ten times, clients would leave looking visibly lighter than when they first sat down because I'd given them information they couldn't deny was coming from a loved one who had passed away.

FINDING MY VOICE

After several months in the café, the editor of a weekly publication wandered in for a reading and after being "completely blown away," asked if she could do a story on me. Of course I said *YES,* and when her profile became the cover story it put me on the map. My phone started ringing off the hook and that's when I finally opened my own shop.

Once in my new office space, I stopped using automatic writing to channel Spirit. I realized I was using it as a crutch and it was actually holding me back. (Not only that, I worried I'd soon get carpal tunnel syndrome!) Plus, I could tell I was graduating to a new level of communication; instead of simply feeling compelled to write (based on an internal flow of words), I started to notice energy outside and around me. For instance, I would be in the middle of a reading and suddenly I'd become distracted by a spark of light flickering around my client's body. I'd see a flash of a scene, like a car accident, in my mind's eye, or I'd feel a strong tug at my heart, giving me the feeling that my client had a heart problem. Whenever something like this happened, it was hard for me to focus on my automatic writing. Instead of writing down *car accident,* for example, I could more quickly relay that information by saying it out loud. Still, giving up the safety of the pen and paper took faith in my own intuitive power, and as soon as I did, my connection to Spirit got stronger, though the messages didn't always make perfect sense. In the beginning it was trial and error trying to figure out what it all meant, but I'd relay the messages anyway and trust that they were coming to me for a reason. (And this is important for you to understand once you begin your own work. Spirit energy is easy to dismiss, which is why I'll teach you in the following chapters how to interpret and understand the subtleties.)

Hold On! I Don't Get It: Are intuition and Spirit energy the same thing?

Here's the Deal: No, and we will discuss this in detail in Chapter Two: A Different Kind of Self-Help, but for now, think of it this way: Your intuition connects you to Spirit energy, and sometimes, like in the case with Grandma Babe, spirits help us reconnect with our intuitive power. You are born with intuition. It's innate and internal (inside you). Spirit energy is external (operating outside of you). They work hand in hand, but they are separate energies.

What This Means for You: When our minds are cluttered with doubt and fear, it is difficult for us to hear our intuitive voice, which makes it harder to hear Spirit.

Shortly after moving into my new office, a woman and her daughter came in for a reading. I channeled this woman's mother-in-law, who came through with a warning for her son Art to get his heart checked. Hearing this advice, Art's wife and daughter gave each other a look because they knew how much of a skeptic Art was. "He'll never believe it," his wife said. But Art's deceased mother was insistent—something was wrong with her son and if he wasn't careful he would be joining her soon! Art's wife said, *"Okay, okay,"* and promised to relay the message.

Just as she predicted, when she passed the story on to her husband, he said, "So, I'm supposed to listen to this psychic lady for medical advice, now?"

Well, one week later, Art was the emcee for a work event. While on stage, he started feeling bad, excused himself, walked into the nearest bathroom, and collapsed. He was rushed to the hospital and sure enough, doctors discovered a ruptured aortic aneurism. He was immediately taken into surgery and his doctors said there was only a 1 percent chance of him surviving.

Art was in the ICU for weeks. I went to visit him in his weakened state. He cried and thanked me for the warning. He said he was sorry for not listening. I told him that his mother was still with him and helping him pull through. "Your mother assures me that it's not your time to go," I said. After weeks in the ICU, Art started to grow stronger, and after he made a full recovery, he and his family came to me for a follow-up reading. Art said his mother's message was his wake-up call.

HELPING PEOPLE HELP THEMSELVES

As I continued to build my practice, I studied and watched other intuitives and mediums. Some were gifted and some were not, but regardless of their talent, I noticed that many of them had one thing in common: EGO. It seemed as if their "gift" had taken priority over their work. They were using their power to build up their own importance rather than help people in need. This frustrated me. I felt let down, actually.

One night, I sat in a large audience reading by a well-known psychic medium and saw that it was more important for her to be in the spotlight than make meaningful spiritual connections for the people there. From that day forward, I vowed to keep my ego out of my work and have dedicated myself to be used as an instrument for Spirit, nothing more.

Over the years, I've received countless validations from my clients that the information I deliver is accurate. I've seen how the messages that I've passed on to them from their loved ones has restored their faith in a greater power. I've witnessed how repeat clients have healed and reconnected with their own intuitive voice. It's the constant feedback I get from clients old and new that keeps me going. My job is emotionally and physically draining at times, but at the end of the day, I'm grateful to do it. I recognize it as a huge responsibility, and it's one I take very seriously.

✦ TESTIMONIAL

Hi Rebecca,

Numb for the past three years, with the exception of the relentless pain in my heart from my mother's death, it took you just one hour to open the door of acceptance, relief, and absolute comfort for me, my family, and all of my friends who have stood by my side during these trying times . . . You knew names, you knew dates, and you knew objects, as well as events that occurred that only you could know by listening to those who have passed on. You are a very special soul with a very special gift who has the ability to soothe, strengthen, and satisfy! My short time with you was so powerful I could write a whole novel about the experience . . .

With love, as well as gratitude,

Jennifer from Dania Beach, Florida

These days, I see private clients most days during the week and dissuade them from seeing me more than once a year. And here's why: I want to encourage them to start relying on their *own* intuitive power rather than mine. I'm just a messenger. I'm not the answer.

That's why I've developed a program that will allow you to access Spirit all around you, just as I help my clients do during our readings together. (And I'll be honest; my two-year waitlist was part of the motivation here. There's only so much of me to go around!) No one knows us better than we know ourselves, and no one has a clearer connection to our spiritual "cheerleaders" than we do. I know that may be hard for you to believe right now, but we'll get there.

In my darkest days, I was desperate for anything to ease my sense of shame and fear. If I would have known then—before Babe stepped in—that I could get my life back on track by simply going within myself and connecting with my inner intelligence, I could have saved myself many nights of feeling lost, depressed, and out of control. The one consistent message that Spirit delivers loud and clear is that each of our lives is significant, and that it is up to us to make the best and most loving choices to fulfill our purpose in this life. Through my work every day, my faith is restored that we are not alone, that we each have unlimited access to spiritual assistance to give us courage, strength, and hope whatever hard times we are faced with.

Before we move on to Chapter Two, I've created an exercise to help you begin to tap into your intuitive knowing. While it might be tempting to skip ahead, I promise you that this introductory exercise is easy and won't take a lot of your time—five to ten minutes max. Plus, it's a good one to have in your pocket because we'll be building on it later on. I know I said earlier that you have the option of skipping the exercises and coming back to them later, but on second thought, if you read only *one* exercise this first time through, it should be this one. Here's why: Connecting with your intuition starts with quieting your mind chatter, so if that's the only practice you incorporate into your life while reading this book—fantastic! That's an enormous accomplishment because quieting the mind can be a beast of a challenge. Most of us walk around with constant chitchat going on inside our heads. Whether it's thinking about what you'll do next, or why you won't do whatever it is you were *supposed* to do next, your analytical mind likes to take over and dominate. I'm no different, actually, so when I want to quiet the grocery lists, errands, and baby talk, I start with this simple breathing exercise.

Start Breathing

{DO THIS TO QUIET THE MIND AND GET PRESENT}

What you'll need: Five undisturbed minutes. Choose a quiet place where you feel comfortable. For example, sit in the backyard or in a park (or on a bus stop bench, if that's all you have). It doesn't matter where you are, as long as it's an environment that puts you at ease.

Close your eyes and begin to breathe deeply. After a few deep breaths, focus on clearing out your "icky" energy. Take a minute and ask any negative energy that's hanging around to hit the road. Continue to breathe. Notice your breath start to slow down and become a steady flow of inhales and exhales.

Breathe.

For the next five minutes try quieting your mind chatter. Stop thinking about what you're going to do as soon as this exercise is over, how you're going to meet your work deadlines, or what you're going to make for dinner. Release thoughts about yesterday or last week or last year. The goal here is to stop thinking about the past or the future and to learn what it feels like to be present.

Breathe.

Let your worries and anxieties drift away.

How did you do? Was it hard? I bet it was. Like I said, quieting the mind is easier said than done. Our stubborn minds *love* to create resistance. They're experts at it! So, don't beat yourself up if you found this ridiculously difficult to do the first time. It's a concentrated practice and it'll get easier over time. It really will.

This exercise helps me get into a more receptive state of mind for all types of spiritual work, and I encourage you to experiment with it throughout the pages that follow.

2

*

A Different Kind of Self-Help

When I tap into someone's energy, I rely on the spirits around that person to give me insight about what's going on with him or her—mentally, emotionally, and physically. With cues from Spirit, I can see what's holding that person back, and by bringing these issues of unresolved pain and grief to the surface, I'm able to guide my client to start releasing his or her "damage" and move on.

You don't need to rely on me or any other psychic medium to have access to this clarity. The answers are within you. The goal of *Spirited* is to help you wake up your intuition and trust your inner voice. Once that happens, you'll see what I see: the thing that's standing in your way. Then with hard work and discipline, you'll be able to put your past in your past, stop the spinning wheel of worry, and move forward with your life.

We're all born with intuitive knowing. It's our most powerful tool, but most of us barely even know it's there. I like to think of intuition as our internal GPS system—it tells us where we are and where we need to go in life. In this chapter, you will work on turning your system on. That's it. We're just going to focus on turning it on. It's only once your system is up and running, and you're making decisions for your life with more clarity and direction, that you can begin to invite Spirit in for further guidance and enlightenment. So, sit tight. We're not going to ask Spirit to join the party until Chapter Five: Tap the Source. Assuming you *want* to invite Spirit in, of course. If you're feeling a little goosey with all this talk about working with spirit energy, relax. Spirit requires an invitation. Your dead uncle isn't going to just pop up on Thursday with advice about your career. You have to ask him in. How much you open yourself up and develop your spiritual ability is totally up to you. And I don't think I'm bursting any bubbles by saying most of you won't be able to make Spirit connection with the intensity that I do (that is, conversing with the dead on a daily basis) by the end of this book. Like I said earlier, my goal isn't to turn you into a professional medium like myself, but to empower you to tap into your intuitive power and develop a spiritual awareness.

That said, I do think it's important that you have a working knowledge of how mediumship works before you start tapping into your higher self. In this chapter, I'll explain the following:

- What a medium is and does
- How a reading works
- The importance of getting out of your head
- How you can begin to connect intuitively

WHAT IS A MEDIUM, EXACTLY?

First thing's first: A psychic isn't necessarily a medium, but a medium is a psychic. This is an important distinction and a good place to start because I meet clients all the time who misunderstand the difference and confuse the two.

Psychics tune into the energy of people or objects by feeling or sensing elements of their past, their present, and sometimes their future.

Mediums take it a step further. A medium uses his or her psychic (a.k.a. intuitive) abilities to see the past, present, and future events of a person by tuning into the *spirit energy* surrounding that person. While a psychic relies completely on his or her own heightened sensitivity to draw conclusions, a medium gets his or her information primarily and directly from the dead, spirit guides, and angels. The emphasis of my work is making connections with, and delivering messages from, people who are no longer living to those who still are. I like to say that mediums are the bridge between the spiritual and physical worlds. Make sense?

Another important distinction is that while psychic readings often focus on predicting future events, mediums primarily tune into past and present issues. I think future casting, while sometimes helpful, runs the risk of mentally paralyzing people. It can feel very disempowering to be told how your future will unfold—as if you don't have any say in how your life plays out. Well, this just isn't true. You *do* have a say! Despite what any psychic or medium may "see" in your future, you absolutely have the power to design and create the life you want by changing your thoughts and actions (more on this in Chapter Three). This is why I'm personally reluctant to give predictions. That kind of psychic information is usually just insight into what could *potentially* happen based on the road you're currently traveling down, and it should be used only as a guideline to help you make the best choices for yourself.

I Work with the Good Guys

Just like with any profession, mediums have specialties and areas of expertise, so I hope what I say next doesn't disappoint you: I'm not a ghost whisperer. I don't solve heinous crimes or help tormented souls cross over. (Not that there's anything wrong with that. It's just not my thing.)

I work with the good guys—souls that are, for the most part, at peace. Sure, they may have regrets or unresolved issues, but they're not haunted or lost. As it turns out, dark energies aren't attracted to me. I work with peaceful, loving spirits whose main goal is to assist the living. Now maybe you're wondering, *Don't spirits have other things to do than communicate with me? Shouldn't they—you know—move on?*

Ironically, the dead are often trying to help the *living* move on. The spirits around you—usually your deceased loved ones—want you to work through your grief and struggle, so you can have the life you've always dreamed of. Spirit sends messages to give us general guidance, point us in the right direction, comfort us in times of need, help us resolve feelings of loss, and warn us when we are off course or in danger. The loving presence and gentle nudge of Spirit reminds us that we will be okay, giving us the courage to move forward and take that next step in our lives.

Once you're able to accept the existence of spirit energy, you're already acknowledging a bigger picture. And in this picture, you don't have to be alone, confused, stuck, and unsure of your next move. Your life—yes, your life—has a purpose, and my hope is by the end of this book, you'll have a clear idea of what that is.

Hold On! I Don't Get It: What if I'm one of the lucky ones who hasn't lost anyone near and dear to me? Does that make this book irrelevant to my life?

Here's the Deal: Definitely not! First off, while they often work hand in hand, developing your intuitive muscle and becoming aware of a spiritual presence are two separate practices. Because much of the work in the pages that follow will teach you how to connect with your inner voice, this book absolutely applies to you. And second, even if you haven't lost someone close to you (a wonderful thing to be thankful for), you're still surrounded by a spiritual presence that totally has your back. It's true! Every one of us has at least one or two spirit guides who accompany us throughout our lifetime. Stick around. We'll dive into this heady material in Chapter Five: Tap the Source.

What This Means for You: I've sat with thousands of clients who, after understanding that they have loving spirits constantly rooting for them, felt a huge rush of relief and a sense of ease knowing that they weren't wandering around all on their own. They felt lighter, and, for the first time in a long while, even brave.

✦ TESTIMONIAL

Dear Rebecca,

In my reading, you said that my husband's father, Gerald, came through with a strong message for my husband to go to the doctor and get his heart checked. This surprised us because my husband felt in perfect health, but you felt certain that Gerald saw things differently, so my husband went to his doctor in February and had a heart and lung CT scan. It showed several blockages in his heart, but his doctor felt confident they could be easily repaired with an angioplasty. On Monday when they began the procedure, the angiogram showed severe blockages, much worse than the CT scan showed. Two of his major arteries were 99% blocked; another was 90% blocked, and 3 were 75% blocked! My husband is only 54 years old! Both the cardiologist and cardiac surgeon were quite shocked that he hadn't any chest pain or significant symptoms before this—he just felt tired and fatigued. The doctors said he would have dropped dead if he had a heart attack because of the severity and the locations of the blockages. My husband was immediately scheduled for open-heart surgery. I just want you to know that if you had not given us that information I don't think Steve would have gone to the doctor and followed through with the tests. I know you have saved his life. I know all will go well on Thursday because you said he had a long life ahead of him, and because his dad gave him the warning. Thank you, thank you, thank you . . .

   Blessings,
   Nora from Greenwood Village, Colorado

TALKING TO THE DEAD

For communication between the living and the dead to take place, a medium must raise his or her energy and Spirit must slow its energy down. When this happens, we meet somewhere in the middle to carry out a conversation between the physical and nonphysical worlds. How the heck does that work? Well, it all comes down to energy. Energy vibrates and spins at varying speeds depending on how solid an object is. The energy in you and me vibrates at a fairly slow speed because our bodies are dense in nature—and no, by dense I don't mean fat. Flesh, blood, and bone is nearly solid mass, and so our flow of energy is slow compared to that of Spirit, which vibrates at a much higher and faster frequency because it isn't constricted to a physical body. It's free to move around.

Spirit energy surrounds us all the time, so connecting with it is really just a matter of learning how to tap into it. You've probably heard people in my line of work say there is an invisible antenna growing out of your head. It's true. Mine's more like a gigantic satellite.

To raise my psychic energy and tune in, I have to first quiet my mind. I close my eyes and begin to breathe deeply and slowly, similar to the Start Breathing exercise from Chapter One. In addition to concentrating on my breath, I often use visualization to help me stay focused on the present moment and quiet the inner chitchat.

One of my favorite visualization exercises is imagining two radio volume dials on the top of my head. I turn down the dial that is broadcasting the constant mind chatter, things like my to-do list for the day, picking up my son from school on time, replaying a conversation I had yesterday with a girlfriend, and so on. I visualize turning this knob all the way down, so that I can no longer hear any of that distracting noise.

Then I visualize turning up the dial to my higher self—my intuition. As I turn down the mind chatter and turn up my intuitive voice, my energy grows stronger and rises to a higher frequency, like an elevator going to a higher floor. Sometimes my head will spin (no, not like Linda Blair in *The Exorcist*, but more like I've had a little too much wine), my body will tingle, and I will feel lighter, like my energy is floating.

Spirit, on the other hand, must focus and concentrate on slowing its energy down to meet mine. How does this work? Picture a ceiling fan at its highest speed. When the blades of the fan are going around fast, it's nearly impossible to see the individual blades, right? But when the fan is turned to a slower speed, the blades come into focus. Spirit has to do something similar with its energy, so its intended message can come into focus. This is no easy task. It takes a tremendous amount of a spirit's energy and desire to come through, and once it does, Spirit can only sustain it for so long, which is why I have to be alert and on the ready. (It also doesn't hurt to give them a shout-out for all their hard work.)

Hold On! I Don't Get It: You're confusing me with all this talk about "energy." Science is not my strong suit. Can you break it down?

Here's the Deal: What the living and the dead have in common is that they're both made up of energy. In fact, everything in the Universe is made up of energy that never dies, but simply changes form. Let me put it in relative terms: Think about water for a minute. In a cold, thunderous storm, water often forms into hail; while in a blizzard, water becomes wondrous snowflakes that flutter to the ground. In both instances, water has solidified into an icy or nearly solid form, but once it hits the ground and begins to warm up, it turns back into water. Water eventually evaporates into moisture in the air and travels back up into the

A Word about Religion

I leave religion out of my readings and my work because you can tune into your intuitive power and connect with Spirit whatever your personal beliefs are. I've found that bringing religion into the conversation has the potential to separate and alienate people. After countless readings with Spirit, I'm convinced that, in the end, we're all one. We all came from the same place and we'll return to the same place despite our personal beliefs or affiliations in life.

atmosphere and repeats the cycle again . . . and again. So, water changes form, but its essence, or spirit, remains the same. Likewise, our energy changes form when we leave the physical world, but our spirit remains the same. In other words, we never disappear. We continue to exist.

What This Means for You: Your physical body dies, but your spirit lives on. For some of you, the notion that our spirit is eternal may be a little too fantastic to accept. For others, it comes as no big surprise because you believed this all along. Either way, it's not my intention to challenge or validate your belief system, but only to share the messages that Spirit has passed on to me: that our time on Earth is a temporary gift, but our spirit has a permanent residence back "home."

Let's try another water analogy. Imagine the ocean as the place our spirit comes from. Some call this Heaven, Source, Divinity, the Universe. Now imagine a teacup filled with some of that ocean water. That cup represents your physical body and the water inside it represents your spirit. When the cup cracks, or when your body dies, your spirit spills out and returns home.

HOW A READING WORKS

Because spirits no longer have bodies to make gestures or voices to speak, they communicate through telepathy by impressing thoughts and feelings into the mind and body of the medium. This requires the medium to clear his or her mind of all excess mind chatter and stay neutral. I have to shut up, so to speak, so Spirit can do the talking.

Before starting a reading, the first thing I tell clients is that the spirits are running the show. I have no control over who comes through, how clear the messages will be, or how long they'll want to stick around. Because of this, I encourage my clients to stay open and avoid deciding ahead of time who it is they'll hear from and what information they'll hear—the spirit or spirits who come through will sometimes surprise you. I often say, "Surrender your expectations and trust that you will get the message from whom you *need* it."

This is tough for a lot of us because we tend to confuse what we *want* to hear with what we actually *need* to hear—you know, like the classic Rolling Stones song, "You can't always get what you want . . . You get what you need." I've found that Spirit's messages are a combination of what's necessary for us to hear at a particular time mixed with what we're *willing* to hear. I tell clients, "All aspects of your life probably won't be addressed today, but I assure you, Spirit will tell you what you need to hear right now."

On with the reading. I start with a silent prayer for protection, usually something like, "Spirits of love and light, please come through and share with me anything and everything in the highest and best good for my client at this time. Please be loud and clear with your messages and help me accurately interpret the information in a loving, healing way."

Once protected, I have my clients say their names out loud to indicate that the reading is specifically for them. This draws in their loved ones

I *Don't* See Dead People

Early on when I was developing my spiritual connection, I battled with self-doubt. It was hard for me not to compare my particular style of connecting with my peers'. Many mediums claimed that they had the ability to "see" dead people. I wondered, *If I'm not seeing ghostlike apparitions, does that mean I'm not really connecting to Spirit?* (I felt like I was in junior high all over again—I wanted to have the same cool hairstyle that all the popular girls had.)

It wasn't until I went to a workshop with Dr. Doreen Virtue, a clairvoyant psychotherapist and author who works with the angelic realm, that I started to feel less competitive and stopped comparing myself to other intuitives. Doreen works with people like me, who believe they have a gift but aren't sure what to do with it. On one particular day, we each had to stand before the group and do an audience-style reading, and I dreaded my turn. *Ack! I wasn't seeing dead people like the popular girls were.* But after ten minutes of making connections with Spirit, Doreen complimented me on how powerful my ability was. Still, I had to ask, "But why can't I see Spirit the way so many others can?" She laughed and said, "Honey, you're sure as heck connecting, regardless of how you do it, so I wouldn't worry so much about the *how,* just know that you *are.*"

From that moment on, I knew that we all connect with Spirit in our own unique way. We just have to figure out what way that is. And that's exactly what I'm going to help you do. (The kicker is that after letting go of my desire to "see," I started to recognize spirit energy as sparks of light, orbs, and swirling wisps across the room.)

It's the strongest energies with the greatest need to make a connection that come through first and tend to dominate the conversation. (Get this— the essence of our personalities stays with us after we leave our bodies. For example, if a loved one was outgoing and a big talker in life, chances are he or she will be the same in death. And the reverse holds true: People who were more reserved, private, or poor communicators are hard to connect with in a reading.) When I see or feel a spirit's energy bouncing around, it means it's excited and has been eagerly awaiting this opportunity to come through.

Once I give my attention over to a specific energy (like a teacher calling on someone in class), my mind will become flooded with a combination of feelings, images, and sounds—mental impressions called Clairs.

Clairvoyance means clear seeing. This is when visions past, present, and future flash through my mind much like a daydream. The images come quickly and subtly, so I must have a quieted and present mind in order to pick them up.

Clairaudience means clear hearing. The irony is that it's anything but clear! This is when I hear words, sounds, or music in my head. Depending on the strength of a spirit's energy, I may hear a subtle sound or an entire phrase. Typically, clairaudience comes from within the mind and not externally. On rare occasions, Spirit will find a way to create an audible sound to get my attention, but this takes a huge amount of its focused energy.

Clairsentience means clear feeling or sensing. Many of us are clairsentient without consciously being aware of it. When we get a strong gut feeling, positive or negative, about someone we just met or when we get the chills for no apparent reason, we may be tuning into the emotional energy of a person or a spirit around us.

Claircognizance means clear knowing. This is when Spirit impresses us with truths that simply pop into our minds from out of nowhere. Claircognizance requires tremendous faith because there's often no practical explanation for why we suddenly "know" something.

What Language Do You Speak?

Most of us have one or two dominant Clairs, although we have access to all of them. I have developed all four over the years, and in Chapter Five: Tap the Source, I will teach you to do the same.

and spirit guides. Then I get quiet and open myself up to receive higher energy. Almost immediately I will start to feel spirits in the room, though I never see bodies. Sometimes, but rarely, I'll see an outline or a silhouette of a person from the shoulders up, but most of the time I just see sparks and flashes and swirls of light move around the room. It's the *sense* of the spirit around me that I experience more than anything else.

Using a variety of Clairs, spirits will offer me validations—names, initials, significant dates, and specifics on what their personalities were like in life—to prove that it's really them coming through. Once my clients feel certain that they're making a genuine connection with a passed loved one, Spirit will usually offer a deeper and more universal message. This is when spirits express regrets or loving sentiments and provide closure surrounding their death. It's also at this point when Spirit gives guidance like, *quit that job, go to the doctor,* or *dump that guy.*

Some of my clients have asked me, *Does that mean that spirits are always watching us?* The answer is, thankfully, no. Because spirits don't have bodies they can't look at us the way we look at one another. Rather, they tune into our energy and *sense* what we're doing and thinking about. They may get a visual glimpse of what we're up to, kind of like a daydream, but it's not like they're sitting in the corner of the room watching us for an hour. That would creep even me out! They do, however, check in of their own free will. Do we have the right to set boundaries and tell them to leave us alone? Absolutely! Stick around and I'll teach you how to do that.

Also, just because they're now in spirit form doesn't mean they're all-knowing and wise. I want to be super clear about this: The dead don't suddenly have the full scoop on our business. They don't know everything that's going on with us—presently or in the future—unless it's important for them to know because we're either in imminent danger or alerting us to certain information will help us with our soul's growth in the long term. Higher energies, on the other hand, like our spirit guides, can *always* peek into our lives, but I won't get into that until Chapter Five: Tap the Source.

Once the spirits have expressed everything the living need to hear, they pull back their energy and disappear. It's kind of like a cell phone battery that starts to lose its charge. It slowly fades away until it's gone.

Something I should mention: If I'm reading someone who hasn't lost any significant relatives or loved ones, I'll often deliver messages from a combination of their ancestors (people in their lineage) and from their spirit guides. If I can't read someone, it's not because they aren't surrounded by spiritual energy. It's because they're not letting Spirit in. They're skeptical, scared, or resistant for some reason. Remember, Spirit can't come through and help you unless invited.

Lost in Translation

When I make a connection with Spirit, it's critical for me to accurately interpret the information coming through. This isn't always easy to do. It's kind of like playing charades. As anyone who's played the guessing game knows, sometimes it's just plain maddening!

In order to translate messages from Spirit, you have to first develop your special language, or symbolism, that Spirit will use to communicate.

This symbolic language is based on your own frame of reference. My symbols will not be your symbols because the information and opinions I carry around in my head are different from yours. Get it?

For example, when Spirit shows me a giraffe, I translate this as a message of strength. Why? Because I think giraffes are strong and courageous. They literally stick their necks out. You, on the other hand, may feel totally differently about giraffes. If lions make you think of strength, then Spirit will show you the image of a lion to communicate that message. Pretty cool, right?

There are tons of other examples of symbolic interpretation. When I *clairsentiently* feel a tightening sensation or a choking feeling in my chest, I know Spirit is trying to tell me that he or she died from asphyxiation or had a respiratory illness. When I *clairaudiently* hear the song "Tears in Heaven" by Eric Clapton, I know that either my client or the spirit coming through lost an infant or child, because this song is about the death of a child. Spirit uses my references and belief system to communicate directly with me. Although that doesn't mean I always get it right. Case in point:

I once did a reading for a woman whose good girlfriend came through. This spirit showed me a vision of my mother's home-cooked brisket. I was sure this image meant that this spirit loved to cook in life or that brisket had special meaning for my client. I said, "This spirit loved to cook in life. Or maybe she had a special taste for brisket? Or maybe *you* have a special connection with brisket?" None of this clicked with my client. So, as I often do, I told my client to just sit with the information as we moved on, trusting that in time it would make sense. But her friend in spirit was insistent. The brisket reference continued to come up throughout the reading until I realized I was supposed to emphasize the *word* brisket. I asked my client to simply focus on the word itself. Within a split second she gasped. She made the connection. Her friend's last name was Briske. The brisket image was to be used as "proof" that it was indeed Ms. Briske who was with us that day.

A Sampling of My Symbolic Vocabulary with Spirit

Pillow=Dreams

Lemon=Bittersweet situation

Scooby Doo or Snoopy=Pet dog

Garfield=Pet cat

Hawaii on U.S. map=Trip to an island or beach

Rainbow=Hawaii or gay or just a rainbow

My grandma Flo=Someone who's polished, fashionable, hip for their age

Stoplight: Green=go forward or yes; yellow=caution, slow down, or wait before acting; Red=stop or no

Wave along=On the right track, keep going

Mountain=At the top of one's game, reached one's peak, success

Flashback to me in Vail or Aspen=Trip to the mountains or home in mountains

Flag=The military, proud of being in the service or has an important flag

Hand or wrist=Wearing special ring, watch, or bracelet

Landline phone=Communication or connection

Cell phone=Spirit has been messing with the phone, strange activity with the phone

Lightbulb on a lamp=Spirit has been messing with the lights

(*Continued*)

Light switch=Spirit has been messing with electrical appliances and wires in the home

Plane=Travel

Passport=Overseas travel

Pumpkin=Halloween or late October, early November

Trivial Pursuit game board=Being pulled in many directions at once, juggling responsibilities, overextended

Box of chocolates or chocolate bar=Chocoholic, sweet tooth, or diabetic

James Dean=Good-looking

Jerry Seinfeld, David Letterman, Jay Leno, Johnny Carson=Comedian, great sense of humor

My dad and grandma's headstones at the grave=Cemetery

Giraffe=Courage, sticking neck out

Eagle=Freedom, soaring

Third eye on forehead/brow area=Psychic/intuitive

Ear=Listen or hear spirit clairaudiently

Zip lips=Keep mouth shut, don't volunteer information or opinion

Pulling hands back=Stay out of it, don't interfere, do nothing

Hands extended=Spirit expressing, "How may I serve you?"

Holding head in hands=A head injury, mental illness, or depression

Spinning, tornado-like image=Intoxicated or very confused

Liquor bottle=Alcoholic

Toasting a glass of wine or beer=Enjoying a drink or congratulations

Suitcases=Emotional baggage

Christmas tree=Holidays, special ornaments, or just a tree

Balloons=Celebration or birthday

Burt Reynolds=Mustache or facial hair

George Burns=Cigar

Ashtray=Quit smoking

Pinocchio=The truth, honesty

Table=Lay it on the table, come clean

My grandpa Harold=Integrity, hard worker to provide for family

Cross, Rosary, or Star of David=Faith or belief in God

Toilet=Plumbing issues

Martha Stewart=Homemaker, crafty or creative

Clock or watch=Divine timing

Nod head=Yes or agree

Shake head side to side, head bowed=Regret, disappointment

Wedding ring=Married, engaged, or it's in the cards to get married

Wedding ring being taken off=Divorce or lost ring

Cobwebs=Clear out old, stuck energy

Boxes=Move or pack up and get rid of things

Feet kicked up=Relaxing or playing

Buddha=Spiritual more than religious, oneness, all religions

(*Continued*)

My dad and a watch=Punctual

My husband or my aunt Connie=Being pokey or always late

Apple=Teacher

Books piled high=Educator, school, or avid reader

Nurse's hat=Caregiver or in health care profession

Rocking/cradling a baby=baby in spirit, either unborn, miscarried, or aborted

Chess game=Strategy

Fabric softener sheets=Laundry

In addition to asking Spirit to be loud and clear and to use my personal symbolism to relay information, I also ask that they provide me with very specific information that holds significance for my client—like the "brisket." Ironically, Spirit will often bring up seemingly *in*significant things to prove that they are indeed present. One example of this is best told in the words of my client Susan:

✦ TESTIMONIAL

On April 15, 2002, my father died at the age of eighty in a nursing home of complications from peripheral vascular disease. He had been admitted the previous December for physical therapy after suffering a heart attack. My three brothers and I watched in dismay as his whole

essence slowly slipped away despite the best efforts of the therapists, nursing staff, my daughter, and myself. I had been his caretaker ever since my mother died in September of 2001. He lived with me for three months, so I was very aware of how rapid and profound his decline was. He went from walking, talking, and driving around town to spending days in bed, barely able to move, talk, or function. My worry was always, "Am I doing enough? What else should I do to help him? What more does he want or need?"

It became clear that he had given up. A week before his death, he was admitted to hospice where they estimated one or two days left to live based on his health history and emaciated state. He hung on for four days. We couldn't understand why he was still hanging on. I was beside myself, fretting and thinking, "Maybe he's not ready. Maybe he does not want to die! Maybe we should be doing more for him, a feeding tube, something!?" I was a wreck. On the day he died, my brothers and I stood in his room and discussed funeral arrangements. The funeral home had asked for any dentures to be sent with the remains. My father had a partial plate with two or three teeth, and it was at my house with all his other belongings. We decided that it was not necessary for me to run home and retrieve it since it did not affect the shape of his mouth.

Also on the evening of my dad's death was Rebecca Rosen's seminar and group reading. Two months prior, my dear friend Amy had purchased tickets for us to attend, and we had been in constant contact the week before my dad died. Amy came and visited my dad's bedside the day before he died. She was dressed in boots and britches since she was on her way to ride her horse at a local barn. She kept telling me not to feel obligated to take the ticket for the seminar and that she would offer it to someone else. I had this feeling that no matter what, I needed to go. I wasn't sure why but I knew it wouldn't hurt to get my mind off the strain and heartbreak of the previous weeks. So, on the evening of my dad's death, I met Rebecca Rosen.

In the seminar, Rebecca spoke of the importance of being clear about our intentions when desiring answers from Spirit. All I wanted to know was if I did what I was supposed to do for my dad. I was so torn with guilt and worry that I didn't do enough for him. Rebecca talked about her work and then proceeded with audience readings. I listened with interest but was still fairly numb from the past days' events, so not much registered. When she was done, she thanked the audience. Then she stopped. "Wait," she said. "There's one more. This is important." She paused. "Someone in here has a deceased loved one's tooth. A tooth or dental device." I raised my hand. "It's a male figure," she confided. "A father figure. He had a very long drawn-out death." I explained the death and the denture. "He wants it. He wants to be buried with the plate," she said. And, "He wants me to tell you that he was ready to go." I thanked God for that message, as it was so much what I needed to hear. She continued, "There's someone else with him, someone with weaker energy." My mom had been weak from her own illness and too sick to recover from her surgery. Her personality was quieter and softer as well. "He's saying there's something happening this month on somebody's birthday." My father's funeral was set to be on my brother Phil's birthday! Then, "Who's the horseback rider?" Amy was in the audience with me, and this was what my dad remembered from her last visit with him. It was his way of acknowledging her. Most importantly, my dad was able to come through just four hours after his physical departure from Earth, and relay the important messages to me that he was safe, with Mom, finally at peace, and that he was ready. And of course my father's sense of humor came through, stating that he wanted his tooth put back in place with his body! Hearing all of these messages made it possible for us to get through the strain of my father's funeral. Anytime one of us started to break down and cry, another would remind us . . . "Tooooooth!" and we would laugh. Dad wanted it that way.

· · ·

IN SUSAN'S CASE, her father came through to ease her grief and guilt around his death, to validate that he was still "alive" in spirit, and to encourage her to move forward with her life. These were all messages that Susan needed to hear, and was open to hearing. As I mentioned earlier, once you begin your own spirit work, it will be important for you to trust that the messages Spirit brings forth are right for you at that particular time.

All Spirit All the Time?

Many people have asked me if, as a medium, I feel, hear, and see spirits all the time. *Like, are you constantly picking up information about people around you?* No, because that would drive me nuts! Even though my connection to Spirit is like a radio that's always on with no ON or OFF button, I can always control the volume, turning the dial to my higher self down like I do music or background noise. It's my way of saying, *Leave me alone. I'm off the clock.* I may be a medium, but I'm also a regular gal who needs her down time. Still, I have friends and family who are convinced that when we're out socially, I'm "reading" them and just not sharing the information. As if! There's such a thing as too much information, especially when it comes to friends and family. I set boundaries. Just because I have the ability to "tap" into your issues doesn't mean I want to!

Occasionally a stubborn spirit will break through anyway (which can be annoying on one of my self-proclaimed "off" days) with a message he or she wants me to share with the person I'm with. Typically, I don't pass information on unless I know the person will be receptive and open to it. My general policy is to keep my mouth shut. If the person hasn't come to me for a reading, I feel like it's unfair to just dump unexpected information on them. The only time I'll break this rule is if a spirit is really relentless and insistent.

One day a few years ago, I was walking down the street with my mom when a man stopped and asked me what kind of perfume I was wearing. Because this kind of thing happens to me all the time (strangers are always asking me odd questions), I knew it must be related to Spirit and not just some random guy trying to pick me up while I'm with my mom! I told him the name of the perfume and sure enough, he said, "That's the same perfume my mother used to wear." After he walked away, I leaned over to my mom and said, "Her name was Rose." Now I could have shared this information with the man and told him that I sensed his mother all around him, but he was just some guy on the street—it felt inappropriate, so I let it go.

On a different occasion, I met a lawyer named Jon at a party. As he and I stood talking, I noticed the presence of his deceased mother all around me. It was so strong. In fact, she wouldn't leave me alone: impressing me on an intuitive level with her initials, then her name, followed by mental images of her son and the sense of joy and freedom that she wanted to convey to him. Jon asked me what I did for work (*I'm just your friendly neighborhood psychic medium!*) and, fascinated, he launched into a line of questions. Since he seemed so interested in what I did, I finally said, "Jon, is it okay if I offer you some information right now?" Once he gave me the go-ahead, his mother started feeding me messages left and right. It turned out that she had recently died and the grief was still very real for him. As I told him specific details about her life and her death, Jon was moved to tears and extremely grateful. He said it was the first time since her death he felt peace, knowing that she was still with him on some level and that she was not in pain.

MAGICAL THINKING 101

As I said at the beginning of this chapter, connecting to the spiritual world begins with waking up your intuition. Some people are naturally more sensitive and attuned to their intuitive power, but we can all develop and strengthen that muscle if we choose. It's like singing. We all have voices and the ability to sing. Some of us came out of the womb with brilliant voices that needed little, if any, training to perfect. For the rest of us, singing just isn't our thing. But while it may not be our strongest gift, we can still learn to sing better. It's the same with developing your intuition. With focus, discipline, and trust, we all have the power to quiet our minds, go within, and find the answers we've been searching for.

Hold On! I Don't Get It: I think I understand the concept of intuition, but where does it come from? And what happens when I'm "connected" to it?

Here's the Deal: Like I said before, your intuition is innate—you're born with it. It's within you and belongs to you, and at the same time, it's linked to a collective wisdom. (Some people call this Source, God, or the Universe.) When you're connected to your intuition, you can tap into a deeper sense of knowing and clarity about your life and where you fit into the bigger picture. Our intuition helps us better navigate our world. The more in tune we are, the more inclined we are to make better and wiser choices for ourselves. Personally, before I make any decision, I always check in with my intuition.

What This Means for You: To strengthen your intuitive voice, you must get in the habit of clearing all the noise out of your mind. I can't say this enough—the inner chitchat has *got* to go! This will take practice and time, but it's worth it. When we're able to silence our regrets over the past and worries about the future, we start to see our lives in the present with a deeper sense of clarity.

So, LET'S WORK ON quieting your mile-a-minute mind and connecting to that inner voice. We're going to pick up where we left off in Chapter One and expand on that first breathing exercise by adding a visualization meditation. *Meditation?* That's right—meditation. I don't know if you realized, but that's exactly what you were doing back there. You were meditating!

Meditation is just a nice way of asking your mind to shut up. It's the simple act of quieting your mind of all unnecessary chatter, worries, opinions, and judgments. It helps you to stay calm, peaceful, and grounded throughout the day. Meditation also acts as the doorway to our higher self, and despite what you have been led to believe, meditation does not require yoga clothes or a huge amount of your time in some special, sacred room. I know women who meditate in their cars for five minutes before heading into the office—sans chanting, incense, or airy-fairy music. So, get over it—you can do this!

Easy-Peasy Meditations

{DO ANY OF THESE TO QUIET DOWN THE INNER CHITCHAT}

Below is a short list of places and activities where I find meditation occurs not only more easily, but also enjoyably. Pick one that suits you and find a time in the day where you can begin to do it regularly. The idea is to spend five minutes in meditation, calming your mind and focusing on the present. (Just five minutes! That's nothing. You can do anything for five minutes!) Whichever one you choose, begin with your simple breathing exercise from Chapter One.

1) **Get outside.** Breathe. Smell the air. Notice the colors around you. Getting out into the fresh air within a natural setting is an easy and spectacular way to calm the mind. Nature grounds you in your body and clears your stagnant energy. Whether you sit in a city park or your backyard, take a hike, or walk along the beach,

your mind is likely to stop the constant chatter and allow you to be in the present moment.

2) **Take a bath.** A great way to quiet the inner jib-jab is by soaking in a bath sprinkled with sea salt or any other natural, aromatic scent that pleases your senses. Relax into the water and focus on how it feels around your body. It's a simple yet effective way to melt away anything that might be standing between you and your ability to connect intuitively. (Salt is known to cleanse negative energy and water often enhances your intuitive ability, especially if you are an astrological water sign.)

3) **Cook.** Cooking is a love and a passion for many people because it can be both a creative and therapeutic outlet. If the kitchen is a positive space for you—a place where you allow yourself to relax and quiet your mind—then make this one of your meditation spaces. The next time you're preparing a dish, focus on staying present and open to your intuition.

4) **Listen to music.** For many of us, music has a powerful effect on our intuitive and spiritual energy. It can calm, inspire, and uplift us. It often takes us out of our left analytical brain and puts us into our right creative brain. Listen to a piece of music that particularly speaks to you. Focus on a particular note, lyric, or melody. Use this as an opportunity to slow down, quiet your mind, and connect with your higher self.

5) **Move.** When we don't make time to open up our bodies and allow energy to move through us, we tend to get blocked, stressed, and irritable. Inactivity affects our physical and mental health, making it difficult for us to connect intuitively. Physical activities, such as walking,

running, hiking, cycling, swimming, rollerblading, weight training, and yoga, are excellent ways to stay centered and balanced. I like to do yoga postures to help me stay focused on the present. When my mind starts to drift to my to-do list, my postures weaken and I tumble over.

How'd you do?

IF FIVE MINUTES of focused breath and concentration felt hard, it's because it is! But don't give up—keep at it. And for all of you overachievers, let go of any expectations of becoming an expert at quieting your mind overnight. Give yourself a break. This is going to take your ongoing effort and patience. Start by setting aside five minutes a day to do your favorite easy-peasy meditation . . . then ten . . . then fifteen.

Even I still struggle with this from time to time. When I'm feeling distracted and frazzled, I imagine my intuition as a disconnected wire shooting stray sparks here and there. To reconnect, I take a few quiet moments and visualize plugging back into my higher self. I, too, have to be constantly vigilant about shushing my mind. You'll discover that the mind doesn't like to lose control, so it's a constant challenge. With practice and time, I've learned how to quiet down more quickly and trust that my intuitive voice will guide me.

Would it help you to know what my meditation process looks like? No problem. Here's an example of what goes on in my head when I sit down to meditate.

My Meditation Process

I close my eyes, take a few deep inhales through my nose, and exhale through my mouth. My body starts to relax and I mentally tell myself:

Okay, I'm going to "just be" for the next half hour. I say a prayer of thanks: *Thank you Mother, Father, God . . . to all my guides and any spirits present with me now. I invite you in to help clear my mind, body, and soul of any negative or fear-based energy. I am open, willing, and grateful to receive your light, love, and wisdom now. Please show or tell me anything I need to know for my highest good. Thank you and amen.*

I continue to breathe in and out and then a thought will pop in, *I forgot to tell the babysitter about changing the time on Saturday night! Guides, please remind me to do that later! . . . Okay, back to my breath . . .* in and out . . . in and out . . . I visualize my spirit guides standing around me. I feel them lift layers of fearful energy off me . . . *Why did I eat that chocolate last night?! I know better; it's not on my diet! Oops, I disconnected from my guides again. Sorry. Back to you! . . .* breathe . . . in and out . . . I see my guides again and hear them say, "No worries, just breathe and just be." I think about my grandfather in the hospital. *I hope we get out to LA before he decides to cross over! What if it's next week? I can't travel yet with our newborn . . .* I realize I'm off track again . . . *Please go away, meddlesome thoughts. I'm trying to meditate!*

SEE WHAT I MEAN? Silencing the mind is tough, even for me. When we let our minds roam free we're often doing one of the following: thinking about past memories, events, and conversations; or anticipating future events, worrying about what's to come, what needs to be done, wondering how it's going to play out. When we let our minds drift like this, we're not being present.

Fade to Black

When I say "focus on the present," I mean resist conjuring up mental images, like movies in your head, about the past or future. Simply be in

the here and now, attentive to what you can see, hear, smell, and touch—
right in front of you. Right now. Another analogy:

Sometimes when I'm watching TV and my favorite show goes to a
commercial break, there's a dip to black before the commercial starts.
It's like a second or two of nothingness between when my show ends
and the commercial begins. You know what I'm talking about? Well, it's
probably a blip or a mistake of some kind, but I like to think of it this
way: The commercials are like your mind chatter and that frame or two
of black is like the present. That gap of nothingness is what it's like to
be present and have a quieted mind. Your goal in meditation is to park
your mind in the black and stretch out that gap for as long as you can.
You're creating space for silence and stillness. And it's in this space that
you will begin to connect intuitively and open yourself up for spiritual
guidance.

Hold On! I Don't Get It: As much as I try, I can't stop my mind from
racing!

Here's the Deal: For those of you who find yourself going around and
around, feeling trapped by your mind thoughts, don't fret! Turn to page
229 at the back of the book and try the Mind Tricks for Those Who
Can't Stop Thinking. (If this isn't you, then read ahead.)

The Annoying Ego

I hope I haven't given you the wrong impression. The mind isn't all bad.
It's an absolutely necessary and wonderful tool (just try living without
it). It's just that many of us have fallen into the trap of listening to and
being guided by our minds (ego) more than our hearts (intuition).

Negative thoughts and your mind banter tend to be ego-driven *(Am I good enough, smart enough, beautiful enough?).* The person who is stuck in his or her ego tends to operate from the icky place—that part of the mind where fear, doubt, judgment, anger, jealousy, impatience, and anxiety hang out. The egocentric person is typically not very happy when you break it down. That said, the ego's got a lot going for it. It's responsible for our confidence, our sense of self, and our drive. The thing we want to be careful of, then, is spending too much time in our ego. When we're feeling disconnected, dissatisfied, and alone, it's usually because we're not striking a balance between the ego (mind) and our intuitive voice (heart). In Chapter Four: Put Your Past in Your Past, I will show you several ways to create that balance.

STILL A SKEPTIC?

Still having a hard time believing that tapping into intuitive power and a heightened spiritual awareness is even possible? It's perfectly reasonable and normal if you are. As I mentioned, I battled with self-doubt for a *looooonnnnngggg* time. My mind, trained to be analytical, practical, and three-dimensional, constantly got in my way. It wasn't until I finally had my big "Oh my God" moment that I went from part-time skeptic to full-time believer.

My "Oh My God" Moment

Throughout the years I was receiving guidance from my grandma Babe, she'd frequently reference my "soul mate." She repeated the name Ryan, mentioned "a rose," told me his birthday was September 24, and promised me that he would come into my life once I healed myself. It was almost as if Grandma was using him as bait for me to do my healing work.

I admit, I was intrigued, but a dead grandma playing matchmaker? For fear of seeming weird and desperate, I kept those messages to myself and put Babe's mystery man in the back of my mind.

At the end of my senior year in college I went home for the summer to visit my family. Within days of being back in Omaha, Mom suggested setting me up with a guy she'd met who was my age. *Please—first my dead grandma and now my mother!* I dismissed the idea at first, but when a family friend also gave him the thumbs up, I relented. A summer romance did sound kind of fun.

So, I decided to give this Brian Rosen a call soon after and we made arrangements to meet. As I lay in bed the night before our date, I thought about Grandma Babe's mention of "my Ryan" and considered that maybe Ryan was actually Brian. But I stopped myself before I read too much into the name. I hadn't even met the guy!

That night, I had a dream. In it, a man asked me what my favorite number was and I instinctively said, "The number eight." When he asked why I said, "Because eight turned sideways is the symbol of infinity." He replied, "Well, then eight is my favorite number, too." After that, we looked into each other's eyes with an unspoken knowing that we were meant to be together. *Sappy, right?* Hold on—it gets worse.

The next morning when I woke up, I jumped out of bed, grabbed my journal, and furiously wrote every detail of my dream, still in awe of how real it had seemed.

Later, when Brian walked into the bar where I was waiting, we locked eyes and instantly recognized each other (and, yes, I realize how corny this sounds, but it really did happen this way). For the next hour, we sat and talked like we'd known each other for years. We decided to go out again the next night, and so Brian took me to a baseball game. From the opening pitch, we got lost in conversation and ignored the game. Halfway through the fifth inning, he said, "What's your favorite number?" I nearly choked on my soft pretzel. With a weird look on my face, I slowly replied, "Eight." Then he asked, "Why?" My heart started to race because I knew that this was either some big cosmic joke or . . . was Brian my soul mate? I answered his question the way I did in the dream, "Because eight is the symbol of infinity." I clenched my teeth, waiting for him to respond. When he said, "Then it's my favorite number, too," I looked at him in shock. *No way!* As crazy and amazing as this was, I knew it was probably too weird to dump on him just yet. But then things got even weirder . . .

After the game, Brian suggested we take a walk around the Con-Agra Park and fountain. As we walked, I couldn't get the "infinity" conversation out of my head. Soon we noticed another couple about ten feet ahead of us, and it was obvious that they also were on a date by the sound of their get-to-know-you conversation. At one point, the girl said to the guy, "My favorite number is eight because when you turn it sideways it's the symbol for infinity." *Twilight Zone!* Brian and I looked at each other in complete disbelief. He said to me, "Did she just say what I *think* she did?" I had chills all over my body and I told him I had to sit down. We found a bench and I decided to share my story with him right then and there.

It was a bold move on my part, but I figured if he was scared off, then it would quickly confirm that he was NOT my soul mate—and that it had all been some bizarre coincidence. But that didn't happen. He listened intently and when I was finished, he said he knew I was "the one" for him. That's when I freaked out, in no small part because of how fast things were moving. But I also thought if this guy turns out to be my soul mate, then that means—*no joke*—I truly *am* receiving divine guidance from the spirit world.

That night when I got home, I furiously skimmed back through my old journals in search of the earlier messages that I'd channeled from Babe. I came across her little clues about "Ryan" and the "rose" he would give me. I was still puzzled because he was "Brian" not "Ryan" . . . and then as I mentally repeated his full name in my head, I froze. Brian Rosen. Ryan Rose. I continued to scan back through my journals determined to find something to prove this wrong. *Eureka!* I found a mention of Ryan-with-a-Rose's birthday: September 24. Even though we'd already had our share of strangeness for one night, I called Brian up and flat out asked, "Is your birthday September 24?" He let out a nervous laugh and said, "Rebecca, are you stalking me?" And what do you think he said next? He confirmed that, yes, his birthday was September 24.

Your "Oh My God" Moment

I share this story with you because for me, this was the big event that finally cleared up my lingering doubts about my intuitive power. Of course, the meaningful connection I'd made with Grandma Babe also validated my psychic ability, but meeting Brian really sealed the deal. My trust finally won out over my doubt, and this is what I eventually hope for you. You, too, have a direct line to intuitive clarity and spiritual guidance, and over time with concentrated practice, you will notice events in your life lining up. Now I can't promise you that after you begin these efforts you will meet your soul mate—although, you might! We all have different work to do in our lifetimes and mine was to learn how to stop the cycle of sacrificing my voice and stifling my feelings in an attempt to keep everyone else happy and comfortable. Only after I learned to love myself did Brian enter my life—just like Babe said he would.

In Chapter Three: What's Your Damage?, I'm going to show you how to take an inventory of where you are in your life. I'll walk you through the process of identifying where you are stuck and what you need to do to start living a fulfilled and purpose-driven life. So, to prepare for that, try the following meditation: Get Grounded and Plug In.

MEDITATION

Get Grounded and Plug In

What you'll need: Five undisturbed minutes. A place to sit quietly.

Begin by closing your eyes and becoming aware of the rhythm of your breath—just let it slow down. (As you're starting to see, your breath is the most important focus to meditation. Your breath connects you to your higher self. There's nothing more complicated about it. Slowly breathe in through your nose and exhale through your mouth. Imagine all your worries, fears, and mind chatter flowing out of you with each exhalation.) For the next five minutes try to quiet your mind and focus on the present. Don't be in a hurry. Remember—this is *you* doing *your* work. Try to release thoughts about the past or the future. Concentrate on your breath and on feeling calm and completely present.

In your Mind's Eye, imagine that you have an hourglass figure—if you're lucky, your *actual* hourglass figure! Think of the top of your body as a wide open funnel, able to let intuition in; your middle core as the strong and supportive piece; and the bottom portion of your body as a full skirt sweeping wide around you, grounding you firmly into the Earth. When we get our minds into a balanced state, this is what our *energy body* looks like—open on top, strong in the middle, and grounded on the bottom.

As you breathe, slowly and deeply, visualize yourself as your favorite tree. (I like to imagine myself as a strong and mighty oak.) Your branches reach out above, your trunk is straight and strong, and your roots stretch deeply into the ground.

Breathe in through your branches.

Imagine the warm sun filling you up. Take a breath right down through your trunk and breathe out strongly through your roots, deep into the ground. Now breathe in from the Earth through your roots and draw the breath back up through your trunk and all the way through your branches—out into the fresh air and sun.

Take another breath in through your branches, allowing the sun to fill you up, and again take the breath right down through your trunk and breathe out powerfully through your roots, deep into the Earth.

Again, breathe in from the Earth. Now imagine a current of dynamic white light running up through your branches and reaching toward a magnetic light storm above that symbolizes your intuitive power. Concentrate on this image and continue to breathe.

Repeat these two breathing sequences for a few minutes.

Once you feel like you've really gotten into the mind-set—after five minutes or fifteen, whatever you need—gradually let the visualization fade and feel yourself deeply rooted into the Earth and centered in your body, your central column now a clear channel for energy to flow in and out of, and your mind wide open and receptive to intuitive clarity.

3

*

What's Your Damage?

So, enough about me . . . now about YOU! It's time to move on to headier stuff. I truly know that our purpose in life—each one of us—is to repair and restore our inherently loving and pure souls. On a larger and much grander scale, I've come to believe that our purpose is to help heal the soul of the world. No biggie, right? But seriously, don't worry—one thing at a time. Before we can do the "big" work, we have to fix ourselves. It's just that simple.

After countless conversations with Spirit and my clients, I now understand that every obstacle in our life presents us with an opportunity to grow on a soul level. For me, the Night Prowler provided the push I needed to stop sleepwalking through life. It wasn't until I woke up, saw my life clearly, and did the work to heal that I was able to begin helping others. Every challenging situation we encounter has a lesson to offer us. And until we learn the lesson, we will be presented with the same challenge, manifested in different ways, over and over again. Did you ever see the movie *Groundhog Day* where Bill Murray keeps waking up to the same day until he gets his act together and breaks the cycle? Our spiritual life is kind of like that.

The work I do with Spirit gives me the ability to pick out and actually name the negative energy that is weighing a client down—most often unconsciously—and preventing him from reaching his personal potential. You, too, have the power to identify where you are spiritually stuck and how this *stickiness*, or negative energy, is manifesting in your daily life. You just didn't know it! Once you're able to see where you're blocked, I'll work with you to change your attitude and thoughts around that blockage, so that you can start releasing it. Did you know that just by adjusting how you *think* about your life, you can *create* the life you've always wanted for yourself? It's true.

Clients routinely contact me days, weeks, sometimes even months after a reading to tell me how light they feel, like a weight has been lifted off their chest. I want to empower you to experience that sense of weightlessness and freedom. Sound good? In this chapter, you'll use your growing sense of intuition to:

- Take an inventory of your life and name the thing that's got you stuck
- Identify the difference between healthy and toxic experiences in your life
- Identify the difference between healthy and toxic people in your life
- Learn how to use the power of co-creation to live the life you want!

TAKE AN INVENTORY

Getting unstuck is a delicate process of peeling back the layers of our subconscious to find the root of our struggle, so we're going to take it easy and slow. The first step is to become aware of where your life feels off-track. I want you to think about any aspect of your life you don't particularly like and you're hoping to change.

To get started, ask yourself, *Is there anything in my life that feels difficult, unresolved, or frustrating?* For example, maybe you're suffering from relationship issues, job anxiety, body image concerns, or money problems. Take a few minutes and think about this. Quiet your mind and invite intuitive clarity in. If you're not sure at this point that you've gotten the hang of it yet, no problem. For now, just focus on shushing your inner dialogue.

Some of you will be able to name your struggle very easily, while others might be thinking: *I have no idea what* specifically *is wrong. I just know something isn't right!* If that's you—that's totally okay. If you already had all the answers you wouldn't be reading this book, right?

If the cause of your discontent isn't easy to pinpoint, think about the *feeling* that's got you down. For example, on a regular day do you feel scared, sad, angry, frustrated, resentful, guilty, isolated, or insecure? Concentrate on that negative feeling for now. By the way, it's normal for us to have a range of emotions or worries on any given day, so focus on the feeling that dominates your thoughts. Is there a particular negative emotion that continues to pop up again and again? You can even jot down whatever comes to mind on a piece of paper.

Give this your concentrated thought before reading on. In fact, you might want to dog-ear this page and come back to it once you've gained some clarity. I'll be here when you do, so take your time.

READY TO PUSH AHEAD?

EXERCISE

Intention Lists

Okay! Next, you'll be taking a detailed inventory of where you are and where you want to be. I really want you to approach this next exercise without judgment or editorial comment. Try not to assign a good or a bad value to anything you write down—that's just your ego talking. Before you start the following intention lists, take a few slow and deep breaths and quiet your mind (remember, your concentrated breath connects you to your intuition). Write your answers on the lines provided below or on a piece of paper. This is an exercise that you can return to at different stages of your life when you want to check in on where you are now and where you want to go next.

REALITY LIST ∽ *Here's Where I Am*

Make a list of what your current life looks like. Write whatever comes to mind about where you are now—physically, mentally, emotionally, and spiritually. Write down the positive and the negative. This list can be a combination of feelings, situations, and people in your present reality. It might look something like this: *Happily married, in good health, struggling at my job, feeling resentment toward a coworker, huge credit card debt . . .*

Try to remove the personal attachment to your story and describe your life objectively, like you're looking at yourself from the outside. This is easier said than done, so breathe and take it slow. It takes a tremendous amount of courage to honestly look at who and where you are, but you found this book and it found you, so I know you're ready to do the work. That is not to say that every step of it will be fun. In fact, it might feel superbly awful, but uncovering the gunk is the first part of the healing process. In other words, you can't get clean without getting a little dirty first.

Reality List: Here's where I *am*

_____

_____

_____

_____

_____

_____

_____

_____

_____

_____

_____

WISH LIST ↣ _Here's Where I Want to Be_

Next, shift your focus and fantasize! Imagine amazing things coming your way. If you could have everything you ever wanted, what would your life look like? Your list might read something like this: _I want a bigger house, a new career, to find the love of my life, lose that last ten pounds . . ._

It's our tendency to list material and cosmetic wealth when describing our "perfect" life, and this is an absolutely acceptable thing to do (because in many cases, a new house and a better job _would_ make our lives feel a whole lot better!). But in addition to listing items or circumstances, write down how having these things would make you _feel_. For example, would a better job make you feel more successful? Fulfilled? Creatively inspired? Secure? You see, it's often the positive feeling we crave rather than the material object that inspires the feeling. You feel me?

Wish List: Here's where I want to _be_

_____

_____

_____

_____

_____

_____

_____

_____

_____

_____

_____

_____

_____

DUMP LIST ∽ *Here's What I Want to Get Rid Of*

Look back at your Reality List and transfer the things that you want to get rid of onto your Dump List. Negative feelings go on this next list (grief, anger, depression), as well as unhealthy situations (job dissatisfaction, unlucky in love, money issues). Put your "drug of choice" on this list, too (food, alcohol, cigarettes, compulsive shopping, controlling tendencies, or excessive exercise—anything you use to escape or numb a pain), plus toxic people who drain your energy or make you feel bad about yourself. (This doesn't mean you will necessarily *dump* these people. I'll discuss the effects and how to handle "psychic vampires" later in the chapter. For now, put down anyone that makes you crazy.)

If you're not sure what to put on the list, close your eyes and mentally ask your intuitive voice, *Who or what in my life is not serving me well? Who or what is draining my energy or holding me back from being my highest self?* Let images of people, situations, substances, etc., come to mind and then, without editing these images, open your eyes and write them down. Again, try not to judge or overanalyze what comes to mind. This is probably the hardest list to write because it requires you to face things you might have been avoiding. Be brave. It's going to pay off—I guarantee it.

Dump List: Here's what I want to *take out*

_____

_____

_____

_____

_____

_____

_____

_____

_____

KEEPER LIST ☙ *Here's What I Want to Keep*

Now for some positive stuff! The Keeper List includes everything in your life that feels good. Who makes you feel charged and energized? What activities fill you up and inspire you? What do you like about yourself? List everything you are grateful for. Take some time here and focus on the positive. Have fun!

Keeper List: Here's what I have to *be grateful for*

_____

_____

_____

_____

_____

_____

_____

_____

_____

_____

_____

_____

_____

You're not coming up blank, are you? There's got to be a few things you like about your life and want to keep! It's our tendency to focus on what's *not* working and skip over the good stuff, but when we take time to focus on the gifts we already have, we attract more good things into our life experience. When we're in a place of gratitude, our lives will start to unfold more easily, bringing people and situations to us that help us reach our highest purpose and potential. I'll be showing you how to get there. In the meantime, try my habit of saying, "Thank you, thank you, thank you," under your breath throughout the day, or make up your own mantra of gratitude and try integrating it into your daily routine. (What's a mantra? It's a Hindu term, and it's basically a special saying or prayer that holds significance and meaning for you. I have two favorite simple mantras: *Just be* and *Let go, let God.*)

WHEW! IF YOU'VE MADE it this far, take a moment to pat yourself on the back. This isn't easy stuff. Dissecting your life can feel very uncomfortable. Don't be surprised if you're experiencing a mixed bag of emotions right now—anger, sadness, guilt, regret, and confusion. To top it off, writing it all down probably left you feeling more vulnerable and exposed than you prefer to be. But unless someone is standing behind you reading over your shoulder, the only person taking a close-up look at your life is you. Still, mirrors can be brutal. If completing the Intention Lists left you feeling a little wobbly, turn to the Let Go and Fill Up meditation on page 232 at the back of the book. It will help you physically let go of any negative energy so you can replace it with positive energy. When we're full of positive energy, we have less room for the nasty stuff to come creeping back in. Makes sense, right?

If you're not in the mood for another meditation right now, then simply take a break. Mark this page and come back to it when you're refreshed and revived. In the next section, you'll need your energy to begin the work of replacing your Reality List with your Wish List.

MY STRUGGLE IS YOUR STRUGGLE

Now that you have a deeper sense of what feels good about your life and what doesn't, I want you to take a look at the chart on the next page. Over the years, I've compiled a list of the struggles that come up most often in my sessions, and how they commonly manifest in our day-to-day lives. Some of them might seem obvious (like, *I can't lose the last ten pounds because I have an issue with weight*—duh!), but I've included this chart for two important reasons: One, because you might recognize yourself in it, triggering some truth you've been afraid to admit; and, two, to give you a shot of courage. The simple truth is that you're not alone. What you're wrestling with is probably very similar to what someone five doors down . . . five stories up . . . and five blocks away is battling, too.

1) MANIFESTATION/DAY-TO-DAY	2) STRUGGLE/ISSUE
I eat for comfort rather than hunger.	Emotional eating
I can't seem to lose these last ten lbs.	Weight issue
I'm anorexic.	Weight issue
I'm obese.	Weight issue
I overeat, abuse drugs and/or alcohol, chain smoke, to numb anxiety.	Unhappy in career
I use drugs/alcohol/cigarettes to numb my pain/anxiety.	Addiction issue
I fill my void with material things or substance abuse.	Unclear on life purpose
I'm always struggling financially.	Money issue
I hate my job but can't leave it.	Job issue
I'm always in debt.	Money issue
I can't seem to advance and earn more money in my career.	Career plateau
I'm a compulsive shopper/spender.	Money issue
I'm always sabotaging good relationships.	Relationship issue
I choose unavailable guys/girls to date.	Relationship Issue
I'm unfaithful in my relationships.	Loyalty/dishonesty issue
I'm very guarded with my feelings in all my relationships.	Relationship issue
I attract unhealthy relationships and feel unappreciated.	Insecure and low self-worth
I have no patience for needy people/relationships and cut them out.	Relationship issue
I'm having an affair with a married man/woman.	Lonely and unhappy marriage
I'm overly controlling with my child.	Power struggle
I'm afraid to speak up to my husband/wife.	Authority issue
I'm judgmental, critical, and negative.	Attitude issue
I'm short-tempered with my family/spouse, yelling too often.	Family issue

1) MANIFESTATION/DAY-TO-DAY	2) STRUGGLE/ISSUE
I gossip about people excessively to win friends.	Insecurity issue
I guilt-trip my family and friends.	Passive/aggressive issue
I often hear myself being critical of and complaining about other people.	Judgmental/critical
I find myself always apologizing or feeling wrong.	Chronic guilt
I have insomnia and my mind races with anxiety.	Sleep issue
I'm unable to get pregnant/miscarrying.	Infertility issue
I get several colds a year.	Chronic illness/self sabotage
I have constant migraines.	Health issue
I'm always getting sick.	Health issue
I feel burned out or exhausted.	Job issue
I lie in bed all day or never leave my house.	Depression
I have too many car accidents and other minor daily accidents.	Accidents
I swallow my feelings and let this dis-ease reside in my body.	Confrontation fear
I never pass the audition/I never get the part.	Career issue
I'm scattered, unorganized, and unproductive.	Self-destructive habits, behaviors
I'm a perfectionist and must be number one with everything I do.	Competition issue
My home has been on the market forever!	House/real estate issue
I can't get past the death of a loved one.	Grief

As you can see, there's only a subtle distinction between what your struggle or issue is and how it's reflected through your everyday actions. For example, my struggle with emotional eating played out by stuffing myself full of comfort food when I wasn't hungry—and in my sleep, no less!

Study the list for a few more minutes. Anything ring true for you? Do you know what your issue is and how it could be manifesting in your life? Maybe it's still unclear. That's okay. Let's dig a little deeper.

What's in Your Spin Cycle?

Think of your spin cycle as how your issue continues to show up day to day. In this section, you'll work at identifying any recurring and unresolved patterns in your life. I'll be here to help. Through the years, Spirit has guided me to pinpoint unhealthy patterns for clients who, in many cases, were totally unconscious of their repetitive behavior.

I once did a reading for a woman who seemed to have everything going for her—great job, financial stability, perfect health—but she was in one bad relationship after another. She attracted men into her life who were verbally abusive, dismissive, and unkind, but she didn't know why. Then, in a reading with me, her father in spirit came through and apologized for ignoring her as a child and mistreating her. That's when she made the connection! It wasn't until she could forgive her father and release the abusive memory of him that she started to attract partners who valued her.

In another reading, a female client complained about always suffering from allergies or getting colds and the flu. Her spirit guide came through and explained that she was unconsciously punishing herself for aborting a baby when she was a teenager. Until she forgave herself, she would continue to make herself sick.

Spin Cycle

You can look at what's in your spin cycle in a number of ways. The only thing that's non-negotiable is that you stay open and honest. I want you to look for repetitive patterns in your life that could be outward manifestations of an inner spiritual block.

But first, let's start with the good stuff. As you do the work of uncovering your struggle, it's important to remind yourself of your successes. So, think about what comes easy for you over and over again. What aspects of your life require little effort? Making friends? Making money? Making good decisions? Staying in shape? Landing good jobs? Write them down here:

_____

_____

_____

_____

_____

_____

_____

_____

Now, give some thought to what seems to be a constant *struggle* for you. For example:

I always have a steady job, but never get promoted.

I seem to date needy people.

I'm always in debt.

I have a lot of friends, but tend to feel lonely.

Despite my efforts to be grateful and positive, I find myself always complaining and focusing on the negative.

I go out of my way to be social but never seem to find lasting and meaningful friendships.

I set the intention to be patient and loving with my children, but instead I yell and nag more than anything else.

I've developed a real talent and want to share it with the world, but I never do anything to make that happen.

Anything sound familiar? Think about what issues tend to dominate your mind when you don't want them to. What do you find yourself fretting about every single day—sometimes multiple times a day?

———————————————————————————

———————————————————————————

———————————————————————————

———————————————————————————

———————————————————————————

———————————————————————————

———————————————————————————

_____

_____

If you're not ready to write anything here, try one or a combination of the following and I bet that within a couple of days, you'll have a much better idea:

- Meditate. Go within and ask for intuitive clarity.
- Journal your thoughts while staying open for insights to emerge.
- Talk honestly with a trusted friend or a therapist.
- Carry around a voice recorder. Record any recurring thoughts that make you uneasy, frustrated, or fearful.

Another exercise you can do to trigger insight is to create a pie chart divided up into sections that represent the different areas of your life. The categories could be: Family, Friends, Physical Health, Career, Hobbies, Play & Fun, Spirituality, Love. The percentage of attention (your time and energy) devoted to each section will indicate where you have any imbalance. If the chart doesn't reflect the life you want for yourself, it can help you reset your priorities.

The goal with these exercises is to identify the area, or areas, in your life where you have recurring struggle. At this point, it's not important to know _why_ you're struggling. Right now, you just want to give it a name. (In Chapter Four: Put Your Past in Your Past, we'll identify the _root_, or the why, of your issue.)

If you're still feeling blocked, don't be discouraged. The answers won't necessarily come easily. Remember what I said about looking in the mirror—it can be a bitch. But as scary as it can be to uncover the truth, it's important for our spiritual growth that we take an honest look around. So, keep your eyes open. Spend some time getting introspective about the major areas in your life. How much time? That's totally up to you. Some of you might need a few days, or a few weeks, to do this work before reading on. Bookmark this page and come back when you're ready. The truth is that you may need to return to these exercises again and again before you begin to see things clearly. And that's okay. This is going to be some of the hardest work you do in this book. Let feelings like sadness, loss, and grief come in. Be curious about these feelings and trust that they have shown up to teach you something valuable. You're pulling back the layers of your subconscious and this requires your courage and perseverance. But have no doubt—you *can* do this. You're already more self-aware than you were on page 1, so there's no turning back now.

STOP BLAMING BAD LUCK

Now that you've taken some time to gain clarity on where you feel stuck, frustrated, or unresolved, I want you to start thinking about your struggle in a whole new way. Ready? What if I told you that *you* created everything that has happened, and is happening, in your life right now? That all situations—the positive *and* the negative—are a result of your decisions and actions, inactions and reactions? That you are responsible for every person and situation that has shown up in your life? I bet that might royally offend a lot of you.

I can hear you protesting, "Rebecca, how can it be *my* fault that the housing market is terrible and I can't sell my house? How could I have stopped the uninsured driver who rear-ended my car, leaving me with repairs I can't afford to make? How could I have known that the person I loved most would suddenly get sick and die? Why would I bring cancer on *myself*?"

I need to say this one thing—and please don't throw this book across the room. *You have to stop the blame game and take ownership of your life.* In the situations above, we tend to want to blame circumstance, other people, or big, bad luck instead of taking personal responsibility. You know what happens when we blame? We give our power away. *But it's not my fault!* You're right! But this isn't about who or what is at fault. When we *own* our stuff, we take our power back. Only then can we stop our negative spin cycle and really affect positive change in our lives.

Still there? Great . . . because what I'm about to give you is good news—it really is.

When clients come to me with questions for their passed loved ones about why X, Y, or Z is going wrong in their lives, do you know what I almost always hear back from Spirit? *It might not seem like it right now, but it's happening for a reason—a good reason!*

My years of Spirit work tell me this is true: Every challenge or hardship we face offers us an opportunity to evolve on a soul level. When we choose to find the gifts, or the lesson, in whatever we're struggling with, we take back our power and stop feeling like a victim. If we shift our perception and try to see, like they say, the forest for the trees, and understand how our struggle is helping us spiritually grow, then we pass the test of going through the lesson in the first place!

Hold On! I Don't Get It: What do you mean? What kind of test? And what about the *really* bad stuff, like murder? Are you saying there's a gift in that?

Here's the Deal: What I've learned from Spirit is that there are two reasons why "bad stuff" happens to us on an individual level, and we're the driving force behind both of them. In each case, we set up specific situations to test *ourselves* and learn valuable life lessons. Here's the first: (As for the really, really bad stuff, I'll address that later in Chapter Seven: Let Go.)

The Ego Test, or You Thought It—You Got It

You've probably heard of the Law of Attraction, the concept that like attracts like. It's no gimmick or book-selling trend: It's real. When we continuously put negative energy out into the Universe through our thoughts, feelings, words, and actions, we attract more of that nasty stuff back to ourselves. This is what I mean when I say that we create everything in our lives.

From this page forward, begin to be mindful of the flavor of energy you're putting out into the world each day. Is it bitter or sweet? Your life is a reflection of the energy you broadcast, so put out what you want to get back. Later, we'll work on some exercises to pump up the positive vibes you send out.

Lucky versus Unlucky

Let's consider two types of people: the "lucky" and the "unlucky." For the lucky person, life always seems to be working out. Lucky has a great job, financial stability, a perfect partner, lots of friends, and is often the winner of cool things like free Princess cruises and twenty-pound holiday turkeys.

Unlucky never wins anything. In fact, everything seems to go wrong—her hair never looks good, her boss is a jerk, and her boyfriend cheats on her.

What's the difference between Lucky and Unlucky? Well, it's not luck. Luck has nothing to do with it! It's this: Lucky projects positive energy, says yes to life, and lives in a state of gratitude for what she *does* have. Rather than trying to control every aspect of her life, she trusts in the guidance of her intuitive knowing and lets her life unfold accordingly. Sure, she has her share of grief, setbacks, and frustration, but she doesn't stay focused on them. She looks for the lesson in every situation and then moves on.

Unlucky, on the other hand, operates from her icky place, where she lets fear dictate her actions and decisions. Because Unlucky is often ruled by her ego, disconnected from intuitive wisdom, and focused on what might go wrong, she attracts more negativity—"unlucky" people and events. Unlucky gets in her own way, throwing her life off balance and off course.

The good news for Unlucky is that she can begin to change the circumstances of her life right now, just by shifting her attitude and her thoughts. Going inward and meditating, journaling our intentions, and repeating affirmations of safety, peace, well-being, and love—these are all good tools for redirecting our energy and actions in a positive way. There is undeniable power in the practice of repetition—it helps to script the mind and get our spirit in alignment. Affirmations are statements specifically designed to program a new desired feeling, behavior, or habit into the subconscious mind. Whenever you practice affirmations, you're practicing positive thinking. It's that easy! Try using the affirmations sprinkled throughout the rest of the book to reprogram your inner dialogue. Say them out loud or mentally affirm them throughout the day. Write your favorites down on note cards or Post-its and tack them to your bathroom mirror or office wall. We all have the power to redirect our lives at any moment. If that sounds and feels empowering—it should!

◆ TESTIMONIAL

Dear Rebecca,

I had a series of readings with you over the last seven years and during each session, you helped me tear down walls and realize my own truth. I struggled to understand why I reach for foods and beverages that throw me off my balance—affecting my brain chemistry, mood, and, ultimately, my intuition. Working with you has helped me to realize and differentiate between the toxic energy I choose to surround myself with daily and the human being I ultimately want to be.

Since my first reading with you, I know the work I have done mentally, physically, and spiritually was necessary. Although not an easy task, it feels awesome to be truly connected to Source and embrace it every day.

I love you!

Atour from Ferndale, Michigan

PLACE YOUR ORDER

While we each come into this world with our own set of circumstances, we're also presented with endless choices and opportunities. I sometimes like to compare life with ordering dinner. When we go out to eat, we take a look at the menu and, after careful consideration, we choose the dish that speaks to our present craving and to what we believe will satisfy us best. We give our waiter any special instructions we might have—dressing on the side, salad instead of potatoes. Then we sit back, relax, and patiently wait while our food is being prepared.

I don't know about you, but when I've been specific about my order, I expect that the chef will make it just how I want it and, when it's placed in front of me at the right time, that I will absolutely enjoy it. It would be weird and downright rude for me to follow the waiter back into the kitchen and hover over the chef while he prepared my swordfish, now wouldn't it? He'd probably say something like, "Get out of here and let me do my job. Be patient and trust that I know what I'm doing."

I'm sure you didn't realize that we can follow the same method with our lives: We can place our order (with God, Source, the Universe) and then wait for it to be delivered. What I'm describing here is the act of co-creation, relinquishing the need to have total control over our lives and handing the details over to God. It involves believing that we deserve happiness . . . that the experiences, opportunities, and people who will benefit us most will be delivered at the right time. Does that mean we sit back and just let life happen to us? No, nothing's that easy. Our role and responsibility in co-creating our lives is asserting what we want for ourselves in the first place. I call this *setting intention for our lives.* We place a deliberate order and this puts action into play. After that we gently back off and trust that our needs will be met.

So, wow, really think about it—*what are you going to order?* What experiences do you want to have in this life? What do you want your life to look like, feel like? Go back to your Wish List. Is it accurate? Do you need to be more specific, add more items to the list? Now is not the time to be wishy-washy!

Does this mean we will always get exactly what we want? No. Remember, we get what we *need* and not necessarily what we want. After we place our order, we have to trust that what is best for our highest truth and healing will be delivered, rather than what our ego thinks is best for us.

Hold On! I Don't Get It: How do we actually place our order?

Here's the Deal: First, get clear on what you want. Many of us are really good about determining what it is we *don't* want. Flip that around— what is it that you *do* want? You need to figure that out first. Then either write it down, talk it out, make a vision board, meditate, or pray on it. It's a powerful thing to physically write your order down or say it out loud, but, most important, how you think and feel about what you're ordering is key. What do I mean? We can talk all day long about what it is we want, but if we don't exude the positive energy that goes along with feeling excitement and gratitude for receiving what we've asked for and believing that it's on the way, it won't show up at our door. We can't lie to the Universe. If you don't believe it's going to show up, it won't. Energy is energy, and we attract whatever energy we're putting out there. You might be thinking, *Well, it's kind of hard to get into a place of feeling I already have something that clearly I don't! Otherwise, I wouldn't be asking for it.* I get that. There are two ways to go about this:

1) Imagine something else that's in your life now that you once desired. It could be your current job, the house you're living in, your new baby, your healthy body. Isn't it a wonderful feeling to have something you once really, really wanted? Sit with those positive feelings of accomplishment, gratitude, and joy, and mentally transfer that energy onto the thing you want now. This exercise puts you in the right vibrational alignment to receive other desired requests.

2) Put the desire out there then let it go. That's right—just let it go. Trust that it will show up and stop thinking about it. Forget about it! Instead, focus on being in a good-feeling place. Do things that make you feel joyful, creative, and loving. By doing this, you open yourself up to receive more positive experiences.

True Stories: Placing Your Order

A client of mine wanted to meet the love of her life and so she wrote out a long list of qualities she imagined that he would possess: what he would look like, what he did for a living, interests he would have, the type of background he'd come from, morals and values, etc. She prayed and meditated on this for months.

Sure enough, she attracted him into her life and he lined up exactly with everything she wanted. But something wasn't quite right—she didn't feel a spark. She realized that while he had all the "perfect" qualities, she wasn't in love with him. So, after breaking off the relationship, she made a different request. Instead of telling the Universe what the love of her life would look like, she focused more on how it would *feel like* to be with him. Just a few months later, she met a man she connected with on a base, soul level and she fell completely in love. He was packaged very differently from what she originally pictured, but he was just right.

What This Means for You: Try not to get too attached to your idea of how events in your life will play out. Instead, place your order and, rather than hanging around the kitchen trying to control the chef, walk away and believe that you will be served soon. I have found that a simple, repetitive prayer of thanks throughout the day helps me resist the desire to control. I say something like, "Thank you, God, for bringing me exactly what I need," or "There's only so much I can control. Here's what I *need* today. Please give me clarity, help, and guidance, and the peace of mind to let the day unfold just like it is meant to. I know positive things are on the way. I surrender!"

As COUNTERINTUITIVE AS it might seem, co-creating your life is dependant on your ability to surrender. This is not the same thing as giving up. For example, maybe you're someone who wants to change your career path. Well, set the deliberate intention that you want a new career and then take steps (research, networking, studying, interviewing) toward reaching your goal. Do everything you can to set it into motion and then hand the final details over to God. When we surrender, we let up on our tendency to micromanage our lives and instead trust that what we need is on the way. That said, be warned! Our ego doesn't like to give up control and can get in the way—it *thinks* it knows what's best for us and is often dead wrong.

Hold On! I Still Don't Get It: I really do think positively. I consciously work hard at broadcasting good energy every day and bad things still happen to me.

Here's the Deal: If the Universe continues to show you closed doors, then you may be testing yourself on a soul level. Remember how I said there are two reasons why bad stuff happens to us? The first was the Ego Test. Here's the second:

The SOUL Test, or The Karmic Contract

What Spirit proves to me daily is that we each come into life with certain lessons to learn in order to spiritually grow and evolve. In fact, these challenges are set *before* we are born into our physical bodies; tests that we will either pass or fail in this lifetime.

I've come to understand that we're all born with a loose script, or blueprint, for our lives. The script is based on lessons we failed to learn the last time we were here and those we're meant to learn this time around. (Am I talking about reincarnation? Yes, and again, my conviction is not grounded in any religious belief—rather, in the thousands of times Spirit has communicated to me that our spirits do not die.) On a soul level—before we were born—we each set up certain events to happen in our lives, but *how* we get there is totally up to us as individuals. Yes, that's what I said. *You* set up your own tests. With the help and counsel of your soul group (and I'll explain what that is later in the chapter), you determined what lessons you needed to learn this go-around. It's kind of like sitting in a counseling session where you review what's been going on in your life up to this point and where you need to go next. After you set up what you need to tackle, that's where "free will" comes in. If you go with the flow—meaning you face challenges head-on and with the intent to resolve them—you will spiritually grow and move ahead. But if you resist learning the lessons life presents, which is what *most* of us do, you will find similar struggles continue to pop up again and again in different ways until you get it right.

I know this might sound a little off the wall, but believe me, I'm witness to this every day. Spirits show up with messages of shame, guilt, and regret, wishing they had lived their lives differently—the same sentiments Grandma Babe shared with me. Spirits urge me to show their loved ones a better way because they have proof that what we don't work out in this life will only follow us into the next.

Hold On! I Don't Get It: What happens if we *don't* learn the lessons we're supposed to learn in this lifetime?

Here's the Deal: Unfortunately, many people "die" before they finish their work on Earth. They then carry their unresolved issues with them into the afterlife. *Talk about baggage!* At that point, they take an inventory of the positive and negative choices they made in life and they're given two options: One, they can either work out their unresolved issues in spirit form by helping a loved one who is still living and who has similar lessons to learn (like my grandmother did for me); or two, they can choose to come back into a physical body and try to master their lessons once and for all.

What This Means for You: The sooner you learn, the better. How do we do this? We start by shushing our ego and allowing our intuition to guide us.

Hold On! I Still Don't Get It: What if I've been ruled by negativity and fear for most of my life and have been failing all my own tests, but now I'm ready to get smart and finally pass them? Is it too late?

Here's the Deal: Not at all. It's never too late to re-create.

What This Means for You: Many of us have regrets about situations we wish we could undo—times in the past where we may have hurt someone we cared about, made foolish personal or professional decisions that negatively affected our lives, or compromised our health in a big way.

While we can't change the past, we are given what I call opportunities to re-do. Let's say you have a good friend who likes to dominate and control you. You're afraid to confront this friend, so she continues to boss you around. Eventually, you grow apart and you don't have to deal with her anymore, but you wish you'd been more honest and courageous. A few years later, you make another friend who reminds you *exactly* of your previous girlfriend. She, too, tries to walk all over you, but this time, you do things differently. You stand up for yourself. By doing so, you neutralize the previous relationship. You've learned your lesson— the value of self-esteem and self-worth—and can move on to the next test life has in store for you.

A lot of situations come up in our lives that we just aren't ready to face. When we turn our back on these opportunities for soul growth, the Universe delivers us another chance to learn our lesson down the road. It's like the expression *You can run, but you can't hide*. We can prolong our learning, but we'll continue to be tested until we pass.

TEAM SPIRIT

In addition to prearranging specific events before we enter life, we also choose a soul group to help us learn and grow in this lifetime. I like to call these guys "Team Spirit." Soul groups typically range from five to one hundred souls. We reincarnate with our soul group, although the whole group doesn't always come back together (some take a break and stay in spirit form until the next opportunity to reincarnate comes along). Those souls who choose to come back at the same time do so to help one another spiritually evolve.

If this sounds like mind-blowing stuff, it's because it is. At least it was for me at first. My understanding of how Team Spirit works has come to me through dreams, meditation, and readings, but I didn't finally get it until I read Dr. Michael Newton's validating books, *Journey of Souls* and *Destiny of Souls*.

Just like on any team, some players, or souls, hold key positions. These soul mates, a group of fifteen to twenty-five souls, make up your inner circle. You heard that right—you have more than one soul mate. In fact, you may have several! These are your immediate family members, spouses, closest friends, and anyone with whom you feel a strong and

lasting bond. You feel super connected to your inner circle and that's because you have similar lessons to learn in this lifetime (my grandmother,
father, and I, for example). Are you with me so far? Here's where it gets
even crazier: Each time we reincarnate together, we play different roles in
one another's lives. For example, your husband in this life may have been
your father in another life—or vice versa. Sometimes these relationships
are nurturing and healthy. Sometimes they're dreadfully difficult. Just
because your sister, for example, is a soul mate doesn't mean that your
relationship is a good one. In fact, it might be full of strife and struggle.
It's very common for our soul mates to challenge us, and we them. Sometimes the most powerful and life-changing lessons and relationships are
the painful ones. In the case of my father, his role was instrumental in
pushing me toward self-love and, *boy,* did he make me work for it. But
eventually I learned. I passed my own test and I am grateful to him.

The secondary players are the souls you interact with on a fairly
regular basis, but don't feel as connected to. These are often your extended family members, childhood friends, mentors, and colleagues.
They impact your life, but not as significantly as your soul mates. They
often show up at certain times to help you learn a valuable lesson and
then they drift away. Lastly, the players on the bench are those souls
who are on the periphery of your life. They have a reason for showing
up, but their importance to your spiritual growth is minimal. This reminds me of the saying: Some people are in your life for a season, a reason, or a lifetime. Still, when you meet these souls, you feel an odd
familiarity, like you've known them before.

Psychic Vampires

Of course, not everyone you know belongs to your soul group, but every
person you choose to interact with has the potential of playing a powerful role for you. *How's that?* The people in your life have lessons to teach

you and are also strong indicators of the energy you project out into the world. Do you attract people who are happy, successful, and healthy or the opposite—people who are discontent, defeated, and critical? Part of owning your stuff is taking responsibility for the people who routinely surround you. Remember, like attracts like.

Granted, many people wander into our lives beyond our control. We're thrown into social or professional situations where we're forced to interact with toxic individuals whether we want to or not. We may not be able to avoid these people, but we do have the power to choose how we *react* to them.

In this next exercise, you'll take an inventory of the people in your life and determine whose energy is healthy and whose is not. The goal is to weed out the psychic vampires, the people who drain your spirit and clog your energy channels.

EXERCISE

Weeding Out the Psychic Vampires

Begin with your simple breathing meditation. Close your eyes and go within. Make a mental list of the people in your life. Imagine them sitting in a circle around you. As you shift your focus from one person to the next, connect with the feeling that each one raises in you. What's the first thing that comes to mind? Do you feel happy? Safe? Invigorated? Anxious? Afraid? Depleted? Spend a few minutes meditating on this and then open your eyes and write down the names of the people you've just been thinking about. Jot down the feeling they inspire next to their name. Be brutally honest. (You can always write this on a separate piece of paper and shred it afterward if you're afraid someone's going to see it.)

PERSON   HOW THEY MAKE ME FEEL

_____

_____

_____

_____

_____

_____

_____

_____

_____

If scanning an imaginary circle of people doesn't work for you, pretend each one of them is calling you on the phone. When the phone rings, do you want to pick it up? Think about why you have that reaction.

After you've mentally worked your way around the circle and made notes next to each person's name, sit back and study what you've written down.

Hopefully, you've listed more people who fill you up than drain you, but it's very common for us to have at least one or two people in our lives that "bring the drama" and give us stress. And sometimes, these are people very close to us. So, then what? The purpose of this exercise is not to identify who you need to cut out of your life, because in many cases (like with your mother, boss, or neighbor), you can't! Instead, I want you to become mindful of who does and does not serve you well and then set boundaries around those who aren't healthy to be around. Our ultimate goal is to surround ourselves with people who encourage our higher selves to show up and shine through.

Psychic Shielding

Standing up for yourself takes courage. Women especially tend to put other people's needs ahead of their own. *I know* that one! They often lose themselves or sell out in order to fit in with a particular group or scene. You may feel like it's rude, selfish, or social suicide to limit your interactions with friends and family members who drain you.

But if you don't set boundaries around these people, your energy will be compromised. Ask yourself: *Does this environment or relationship feel good or bad? Is it serving me?* If not, then it's up to YOU to find a way to protect yourself or walk away.

An effective tool for this is psychic shielding, the mental act of visualizing a wall or a bubble of white, violet, or pink light around your body to protect you from lower energy vibrations both physical and nonphysical. In my opinion, this is important to do every day. If you're doing Spirit work or know ahead of time that you will be around large crowds, depressed energy, or someone who is sick, it's an absolutely necessary practice.

MEDITATION

White Light Protection (Psychic Shielding)

What you'll need: Concentration and focus. Other than that, you can do this anywhere and anytime.

Close your eyes and take several deep breaths. Visualize a brilliant white light—brighter than the sun—descending from the crown of your head and slowly expanding all around you, wrapping you in a large bubble of intense, radiant light. As you breathe, the bubble continues to expand in all directions, extending several feet out from your body, shielding you from all negativity and fear-based energy. Mentally invite your passed loved ones, higher spirits, and angels into your day, giving them permission to guide and protect you as needed. You might say:

> Thank you for fully shielding and protecting me today, in a bubble of white light, from all darkness, negativity, and fear I may encounter. Please bounce all negativity off and away from me. Let my white light transform all darkness back into light and love.

As you continue to breathe deeply, see the light now filling your entire being with pure, positive, loving energy. Continue to visualize this protective bubble until you are ready to open your eyes and face the day.

I do this meditation every morning before I get out of bed. (It really takes no time at all.) I hold the vision and set a mental intention to be surrounded by this bubble of safety, light, and love throughout the day. I visualize that any toxic energy I'm about to encounter is unable to penetrate my bubble.

Hold On! I Don't Get It: What if I don't have time to do these meditations every day? I honestly don't have fifteen minutes to spare before noon. Can you give me a super-shortened version that I can use in a pinch—also, a practical application of how this works?

Here's the Deal: Here's a shortcut: Project light! One afternoon a while back, I went to my favorite yoga class, spread my mat out in the middle of the room, and closed my eyes to meditate before class started. All of a sudden, I felt the presence of someone with toxic energy sit down beside me. I opened my eyes just in time to hear her launch into a string of complaints to others around her. (I'm sure you've encountered people like this. I call them your basic downers.) I thought about getting up and moving my mat away from her, but class was about to start, so I just closed my eyes and mentally sent her light. Lots of light! I imagined light pounding down on her, like in a tanning bed. Instead of getting sucked into her dark energy, my strategy was to win her over to me. Well, after about two minutes of this, she suddenly got up and moved as far across the room as she could. HA! Instead of shifting to match my positive energy, she ran. She couldn't take the light.

AFFIRMATION

When I project light, I draw light to me.

What This Means for You: When you choose to transmit positive and pure thoughts, one of two things will happen: Either your psychic vampire will find someone more compatible to suck on, or he or she will be inspired by your positive vibes, stick around, follow your lead, and open up to a different way of thinking.

Hold On! I Still Don't Get It: Are you saying that I should shield myself from and set boundaries around everyone in my life who makes me feel uncomfortable? Shouldn't some feelings be faced and addressed? How do I know if it isn't a lesson or a test?

Here's the Deal: If someone is making me feel uncomfortable, or bad in any way, the first thing I do is ask myself:

1) *What am I specifically feeling about this person and how do I feel when I'm in their presence?* Then, 2) *Is this feeling about me or about them?* If

it's about *me*, I'll usually get an emotional charge in reaction to their behavior or actions, as in, they're really getting on my nerves. This indicates that they're triggering something unhealed within me. For example, if my girlfriend's needy behavior really annoys me, it might be because I have a problem asking people for help. Or maybe I overextend myself emotionally. Or I might judge people who show their weaknesses. Get it? Her neediness and demand for attention are bringing up *my* issues. If we're brave enough, we can treat these uncomfortable situations as opportunities to face ourselves and take some personal responsibility.

If it's about *them*, I generally don't have a big emotional reaction to their behavior. Rather, it's like I'm watching a character in a TV show and deciding whether I like or don't like what I see. If I don't, I can choose to remove myself from the situation. For example, if I'm at a party and another guest is demanding attention by talking over others, gossiping, and laughing a little too loudly, I'm sure to get annoyed. But that's more about *them* and their need to demand the spotlight. I can choose to tune them out or walk away.

And finally, 3) *Is this about me withholding love?* It's our responsibility to be loving, positive examples to those around us if we want to receive that same love in return. If we constantly choose to show up as kind, generous, and loving people, then setting boundaries to protect ourselves won't be necessary because our light will either transform their darkness or drive them away (like the woman in yoga class).

When it comes to projecting positive energy, we can only be responsible for ourselves. We can only do our part and hope others will respond in a similar manner. I've had clients ask me: When I hold up my end of the bargain and my spouse/partner/sibling/parent/best friend doesn't hold up theirs, *then what?*

The following story is a great example of how we can answer this question in two very different ways.

True Stories: Psychic Shielding

I did several readings for a man named Alex, whose parents divorced when he was eight. His mom mentally, emotionally, and physically abused him when his dad left and then sent him to a boys' home to live for a year. She guilt-tripped him, played the victim role, and said she "just couldn't deal with him." Needless to say, Alex and his mother had a difficult relationship through much of his adolescent and teen years.

At age thirty, Alex started going to therapy and began to realize his chronic depression had everything to do with his dysfunctional childhood. His dad had walked out on the family and started a new one without ever looking back, and Alex's mom punished Alex as a way to process her bitterness.

Alex's therapist and I helped him to realize that he didn't need to take his mother's abuse any longer, and that he should confront her. But when he asked his mom to accompany him to a therapy session, she was unwilling to go and resented the invitation. So, Alex decided to put some boundaries up around his mom and focus on his own health and well-being. They didn't speak for over a year. Then Alex's mom started making an effort to get back in touch. She'd begun therapy of her own and asked Alex to come to a session. Hopeful and optimistic, Alex agreed, but once in therapy, his mother's narcissistic and needy behavior came right back to the surface. So, Alex again put up boundaries. He told her he loved her, but that he couldn't have her in his life. *So, what's the long and short of it?* Alex did his part, but his mother didn't do hers. Alex can only control his own behavior, and until his mother does her own work, he has decided to avoid her toxic energy.

True Stories: No Need for Psychic Shielding

Alex's therapy and Spirit work brought up a lot of anger toward his father for abandoning him as a kid, but after healing himself and having his own son, Alex decided that he wanted to forgive his father. He reached out and Alex's dad reached back. They started to build a new relationship. Still, there was some sadness for Alex when they were together—feelings of estrangement and disconnect lingered. Alex wished they were closer, but understood that his dad was only capable of giving so much. Instead of letting his dad's shortcomings affect him in a negative way, Alex decided to transform them into a positive by becoming a more involved father to his *own* son. Because Alex didn't feel drained by his dad, he didn't need to shield himself; he just accepted the relationship for what it was.

AFFIRMATION

I only surround myself with people who make me feel good.

Every one of us contracts certain spiritual lessons to learn throughout the course of our lifetime, are given opportunities that will challenge us to learn and grow. We have free will, so we may not always choose to embrace these situations or recognize why they've shown up in our lives. If we do accept the challenge, we must be willing and committed to do the work so we can free ourselves from our self-destructive behavior and evolve.

The next chapter, Put Your Past in Your Past, is a biggie—you will use your intuition to identify the *root* of your struggle. Digging deep into buried pain, strife, and conflict can be grueling work, but the good news is that underneath all that gunk is the heart of that which you are—a good, loving, and pure spirit who deserves to be happy.

4

✳

Put Your Past in Your Past

Like anything worth having, developing your intuition and gaining clarity is an ongoing practice—one you need to make a personal commitment to. I understand that life gets in the way just about every day, which is why I'll continue to encourage you to establish a pace that works best for you and your life. The point is not how fast you get there, but that you get there eventually. Right?

All this talk about trusting your intuition may sound like risky business, and that's because we're conditioned to trust our minds (what we can see and rationalize) over our hearts. But we each have access to the unseen and powerful energy of our intuition to gain clarity and guide our everyday decisions—though access to this intuition depends on our willingness to use and listen to it. Most of us have second-guessed our inner knowing for so long that we have a hard time believing (or remembering) that it truly exists. When we lose touch with our true selves, we feel disconnected, confused, and uncertain of what our purpose is in life. It's often in this state of personal disconnection that we seek answers and direction from the outside world. The point of this book is that no one knows us better than we know ourselves. In this chapter, as you get more comfortable with your intuition, you'll use it to:

- Identify the root of your struggle
- Release what's holding you back
- Get present

NO MAGIC PILL

Before you dig in and identify what it is that's at the core of your biggest stumbling block, I have to give you my favorite "tough love" speech. Don't worry, it's a short one. Here it is: There's no magic pill.

When I think back on my Night Prowler days, I still get a tight knot in my stomach. Ugh. That was no party, but I'm so grateful today for what I gained. And I'm not talking about the forty pounds, but what I *spiritually* gained from my destructive behavior. My late-night eating ritual forced me to look at *who* I was, *where* I was, and *why* I was behaving the way I was. Had I not gone through that soul-searching process, I would still be stuck there. Staying in a perpetual state of self-loathing is no way to live!

Confronting the truth about ourselves can be scary work, but if you're coming from a place of love, then nothing bad can happen. Don't believe me? I'll show you it's true. The goal of this next exercise is for you to reestablish a loving connection with yourself before you dive into the deeper work.

EXERCISE

Kid at Heart

Do you remember how you felt as a kid, before you wrapped yourself up in layers of armor to protect yourself from the world around you? Do you remember your young innocence? Your trusting nature? Your carefree spirit?

For this exercise, pull out a favorite photo of yourself as a baby, toddler, or young child. Sit with this image of yourself for the next few minutes and notice what feelings come up for you.

Note of Caution: If you are someone who suffered from a physically or emotionally abusive childhood, this exercise might bring up some very scary feelings: terror, shame, guilt, loneliness, anger. If you're not ready to go down that road yet, that's okay. Skip the exercise. If, however, you want to continue and explore those feelings, I suggest you do so with a trusted friend, family member, or therapist present. That way, if you need help getting out of a dark place, you'll have someone to lend a hand.

How do you feel about the little girl or boy in the picture? Do you have feelings of nostalgia? Tenderness? If so, what about who you were *then* do you miss *now*? Look at your eyes, your smile. What do you see? Do you see the spark of intuitive knowing? Jot down any thoughts or feelings that come up for you.

_____

_____

_____

_____

_____

_____

_____

After listening intently to spiritual beings over the years, I understand that our true spirit is reflected in our younger selves. We come into this world with purity, which is not to say we're angelic, saintly, or without even baggage. It just means that we're born with a pure connection to our higher self and to Source, Universe, God. I like to think of it this way: We each have an umbilical cord back "home" through our hearts. If you've ever been around little kids, you've probably noticed that their actions tend to come from a place of love. And that's because kids are motivated by their hearts (okay, and their bellies, too).

AFFIRMATION

I am pure in spirit.

As we get older, fear, doubt, and suspicion often weasel their way into our minds, casting distrust on our once reliable heart. When we stop listening to our hearts, we slowly lose touch with where we came from: a place of pure love.

When I ask clients to look at their childhood photos, I most often hear them say, *I wish I still felt that open and trusting . . . I wish I still believed in magic, in opportunity—that anything was possible . . . I wish I were as lovable and beautiful today as I was then . . .*

The purpose of this exercise is to trigger the deep-down knowing that we're all good, beautiful, and loving spirits. And the person you are today *is* worthy of your tender care. Will you give yourself permission to take care of yourself and your needs? Can you regard your grown-up self with the same amount of softness and caring you feel toward that image from years ago? Try to mentally connect your present self with the person you were then. Imagine closing the gap of time.

Throughout this chapter, I want you to cultivate compassion for the person you are today. Maybe you hang the picture of your kid-self on your refrigerator door, put it next to your bed, slide it into a special journal, or tape it to the side of your computer. Whenever you look at it, remember who you are—a spirit capable of pure love and goodness. I've always liked this quote from Pierre Teilhard de Chardin: "We are not human beings having a spiritual experience. We are spiritual beings having a human experience."

DIG IN

In this section, you'll be going within, peeling back the layers of your past, and identifying the root of your struggle. (If you're still unclear what your struggle is, go back to Chapter Three: What's Your Damage? and spend some more time there. No need to be in hurry. Run your own race!)

"Digging In" is an eight-step process that includes the act of:

- Setting the intention
- Surrendering
- Asking
- Receiving
- Grieving
- Forgiving
- Finding the gifts
- Letting go

This process requires deep meditation, so before you jump in, I suggest you set aside a chunk of time and a quiet space to do the work ahead without interruption. To be perfectly honest, this section could get a little intense. Taking a look at our insides can make the most courageous of us a little bit squeamish. So, take it easy and remember what you're working for: BIGTIME personal growth. You're ready for it!

Hold On! I Don't Get It: Assuming we're able to identify the root of our issue, then what? What if the truth is too scary or painful to handle?

Here's the Deal: Once you begin to dig in, a lot of difficult feelings and realities may come to the surface. If you've been repressing something about your past, it's probably because it hurts too much to face it. I totally get that and understand why you'd rather not feel the pain, but you've really only got two choices:

1) You can do the uncomfortable work now.

Or,

2) You can avoid facing what's at the heart of your struggle, but you'll eventually have to deal with it. If not in this life-time, then in the spiritual realm. Make no mistake about it: Your struggle will follow you. As I've said before, spirits come through with regrets for not dealing with their "stuff" in life: *I'm so sorry . . . I could have made different choices . . . I wish I would have done things differently . . . Don't make the same mistakes I made . . . I regret not doing the right thing.*

What This Means for You: Get ahead of the game and do the work now. Once you shed light on what you've been ignoring or repressing, it no longer has any power over you. You're free!

That said, gaining clarity is kind of like opening up Pandora's box. Once you've uncovered the past, you may need somewhere safe and loving to process your feelings. I encourage many of my clients to work in tandem with a therapist, counselor, life coach, or someone else who can offer support and hold their hand when they're scared. Having strong feelings like anger and grief around your personal discovery is normal and healthy, so honor them by letting them out. Intense emotions serve as validation that you're no longer numb or depressed—you're wide awake. And that's the goal!

Step One: Set the Intention

When doing deep personal work, it's important to be centered in a space of pure love and positive energy. You can do this by setting an intention.

If we mentally set the intention to "be love," only allowing ourselves to receive and send out loving energy, then we don't need to be concerned about attracting lower, fear-based energy that will distract us from discovering our personal truth.

We can set our intention in several different ways, so do whatever feels right for you. Before I do any introspective work, I say a simple protection prayer like this:

> I am rooted and connected in divine love. Thank you (God, Spirit, Source, Universe) for keeping me in a space of love, where I send and receive only love. Please help me to be the highest expression of my self and for my highest healing and highest truth to become clear. I am grateful for my intuitive knowing to guide me and keep me in love's way.

Set your intention and then move on to Step Two.

Step Two: Surrender

Now that you've set the intention to let your highest healing and highest truth become clear, start the work of digging in by surrendering. When we surrender, we stop and take an honest look in the mirror. We look ourselves in the eye and say, *I'm stuck . . . there's something in my life that doesn't feel right . . . I feel unresolved and I NEED SOME HELP HERE!* Remember: Surrendering is not the same as giving up. Surrendering demonstrates our faith and belief that we're co-creating our lives. There's only so much we can control and do on our own and then we have to leave it up to God, Source, the Universe to do the rest. It's like saying, "I need help and guidance beyond my mind's limited perspective." It takes courage to surrender, and by picking up this book, you've already surrendered and freed yourself up for positive change.

Since concentrated breath aligns us with our higher selves and takes us out of our "thinking" minds so we can see the bigger picture, this step involves taking three deep breaths. Set the intention that with each exhale you will release your mind chatter and surrender.

> Mentally affirm on the first breath, "I am willing to let go of all past thoughts and fears that are holding me back."
>
> On the second breath, "I am willing to let go of all mind thoughts and fears that keep me from being fully present."
>
> On the third breath, "I am willing to let go of all future fears and anxieties that may stand in my way of becoming all that I am meant to be."

ONCE YOU FEEL your mind is clear, present, and open, move on to Step Three.

Step Three: Ask (Pray)

Next, ask for clarity. Your quiet mind and open heart will activate your intuition. Meditate for a few minutes on the area in your life where you are struggling (for example, you have an issue with guilt) and how it's manifesting in your everyday life (you're always apologizing for things that aren't your fault). Then ask to be shown the root of your struggle. To help this along, repeat the following prayer aloud (or make up one for yourself that you like better):

I pray for my highest truth and my highest healing to come about now. I ask for my intuition, along with the help of Spirit, to reveal to me the root cause of my suffering, pain, and block.

Spend as much time as you need on this step before moving on. Some might only need thirty seconds in meditative prayer. Others might want to hang out here for half an hour.

When we pray, we give Spirit permission to intervene in our lives. Once we've given Spirit the go-ahead to step in and be present with us, we can take a few mental steps *back* and wait for the answers to become clear. Like surrendering, prayer demonstrates our faith in the unknown, unseen forces in our lives.

Step Four: Receive

This step is the Big Mama of them all, so don't rush it. Continue to breathe deeply as you quiet your mind to hear the voice within you. Spend five minutes to an hour in meditation, long enough to allow insights, memories, and repressed feelings to surface. When you decide to come out of your meditation, write down the answers to any and all of the following:

WHO? Who in my past or present is tied to my issue?

_____

WHAT? What is lying inside of me that I haven't yet resolved?

_____

WHEN? When did these feelings or this pattern begin?

_____

WHERE? Where does it come from? My childhood? The recent past? A past life?

_____

HOW? How long have I carried these feelings/this struggle around?

_____

WHY? Why am I still carrying around this baggage? Does it serve me to hold on to these feelings? Am I willing to let them go?

_____

What you write down might look like scribbled notes, or a list of names and dates. If you still feel blocked, try the following inquiry process. This can be an effective exercise if you're still getting the hang of the intuitive method of gaining clarity. You'll be asking yourself a series of questions to help you trace back to the root of your issue. Follow these examples:

Struggle: I have lung cancer.
Ask yourself: "Why do I have lung cancer?"
Answer: "Because I smoked for twenty-five years."
Ask yourself: "Why did I smoke for twenty-five years?"
Answer: "Because I've had anxiety all my life and it calmed my nerves."
Ask yourself: "Why have I had anxiety?"
Answer: "Because I was mentally and emotionally abused by my father as a child."
BINGO! Root issue.

Struggle: I am seventy-five lbs. overweight.
Ask yourself: "Why am I seventy-five lbs. overweight?"
Answer: "Because I've emotionally eaten for years now."
Ask yourself: "Why (and when) do I emotionally eat?"
Answer: "Because I feel lonely and depressed."
Ask yourself: "Why do I feel lonely and depressed?"

Answer: "Because I have no partner or romance in my life."

Ask yourself: "Why do I have no partner or romance?"

Answer: "Because I am afraid to let love in and allow intimacy."

Ask yourself: "Why am I afraid to let love in and allow intimacy?"

Answer: "Because I watched my parents' dysfunctional relationship while growing up. My dad mentally and emotionally abused my mom."

BINGO! Root issue.

ROOT ISSUE CHART

Below is the chart of common struggles introduced in Chapter Three: What's Your Damage? (I told you it was coming back.) You'll notice I added a new column that identifies the roots of these struggles. Again, this is not a conclusive chart—it's just a guide that highlights the issues I hear spirits most often address. It's only meant to give you examples of what *could* be at the root of your struggle. Take a look and check in with your intuition and ask—*Is this me?*

1) SYMPTOM/ MANIFESTATION	2) STRUGGLE	3) ROOT ISSUE
I eat for comfort rather than hunger.	Emotional eating	Sexual abuse/loneliness
I can't seem to lose these last ten lbs.	Weight issue	Low self-esteem
I'm anorexic.	Weight issue	Ignored as a child/low self-worth
I'm always struggling financially.	Money issue	Low self-worth/grew up in poverty consciousness
I'm obese.	Weight issue	Sexual abuse in childhood
I'm always sabotaging good relationships.	Relationship issue	Fear of intimacy/fear of rejection or abandonment issue

1) SYMPTOM/ MANIFESTATION	2) STRUGGLE	3) ROOT ISSUE
I'm overly controlling with my child.	Power struggle	Powerless in childhood
I'm afraid to speak up to my husband/wife.	Authority issue	Verbal/mental abuse by Dad/ Mom in childhood
I use drugs/alcohol/cigarettes to numb my pain/anxiety.	Addiction issue	Projected fear from parent in childhood, internalized, and acted out
I choose unavailable guys/girls to date.	Relationship issue	Fear of intimacy due to incestuous relationship with parent
I'm unfaithful in my relationships.	Loyalty/ dishonesty issue	Abandonment issue—Dad left Mom for another woman
I have insomnia and my mind races with anxiety.	Sleep issue	Unconscious guilt over death of loved one or death of a situation in past
I'm unable to get pregnant/ miscarrying.	Infertility issue	Shame from past sexual encounters
I'm a compulsive shopper/ spender.	Money issue	Loneliness and purposeless; disconnected from the truth of who we are; spiritual void
I have constant migraines	Health issue	Past life—stabbed in side of head, behind left eye: where pain is now
I'm always getting sick.	Health issue	Resistance to life/fear/ego control
I'm judgmental, critical, and negative.	Attitude issue	Low self-love
I'm short-tempered with my family/spouse, yelling too often.	Family issue/ turmoil	Resentment about being a stay-at-home mom/dad

(*Continued*)

1) SYMPTOM/ MANIFESTATION	2) STRUGGLE	3) ROOT ISSUE
I feel burned out or exhausted.	Job issue	Unmet need for fun and play
I hate my job but can't leave it.	Job issue	Low self-worth
I never pass the audition/I never get the part.	Career issue	(Unconscious) fear of failure
My home has been on the market forever!	House/real estate issue	Fear of change—energetically holding on to it
I'm very guarded with my feelings in all my relationships.	Relationship issue	Emotional abuse as a child
I'm scattered, unorganized, and unproductive.	Self-destructive habits, behaviors	Fear of power due to childhood verbal abuse
I have no patience for needy people/relationships and cut them out.	Relationship Issue	Growing up around narcissistic parent
I gossip about people excessively to win friends.	Insecurity issue	Low/no self-love or self-worth
I fill my void with material things or substance abuse.	Unclear on life purpose	Verbal abuse as child: told not good enough
I'm a perfectionist and must be number one with everything I do.	Competition issue	Self-esteem issue/fear of failure or not being good enough
I lie in bed all day or never leave my house.	Depression	Unresolved grief tied to death of loved one and unconscious guilt about moving on with life
I'm always in debt.	Money issue	Poverty consciousness from childhood/acting out limitations of our parents' consciousness
I guilt-trip my family and friends.	Passive/aggressive issue	Feeling unworthy, unheard, or unloved as a child

1) SYMPTOM/ MANIFESTATION	2) STRUGGLE	3) ROOT ISSUE
I can't get past the death of a loved one.	Grief	No/low self-worth, or abandonment issue—recurring from when Dad/Mom left
I attract unhealthy relationships and feel unappreciated.	Insecure and low self-worth	Born out of wedlock; made to feel like a "mistake" and "unwanted"
I overeat, abuse drugs and/or alcohol, chain smoke, to numb anxiety.	Unhappy in career	Meeting and fulfilling our parents' early demands and expectations rather than our own desires
I get several colds a year.	Chronic illness/ self sabotage	Being sick in childhood was a way to get love and affection
I can't seem to advance and earn more money in my career.	Career plateau	Living under the limitations of our parents' consciousness
I often hear myself being critical of and complaining about other people.	Judgmental/ critical	Others serving as a reflection of us; really complaining about some aspect of yourself
I find myself always apologizing or feeling wrong.	Chronic guilt	Manipulated by guilt as a child; don't respect yourself
I have too many car accidents and other minor daily accidents.	Accidents	Deep-seated guilt and a need to punish ourselves
I swallow my feelings and let this dis-ease reside in my body.	Confrontation fear	Raised in a family where it was not allowed to express anger
I'm always trying to excel at the next thing and prove myself.	Overachiever / busybody	Parents didn't give approval as a child; basing self-worth on external achievements; belief in not being good enough

(Continued)

1) SYMPTOM/ MANIFESTATION	2) STRUGGLE	3) ROOT ISSUE
I'm always feeling tired, drained, bogged down.	Chronic tiredness	Resistance to what is; wishing things were different; a lack of enthusiasm for life
I sponge up other people's negative energy and feel taken advantage of.	Boundary issue	Putting others' needs before our own; raised by a "martyr"; feeling unsafe in saying "no"
I avoid speaking up for myself and end up feeling resentful.	Confrontation issue	In a family where it was not safe to express feelings and truth as a child
I'm often procrastinating or avoiding doing something.	Procrastination issue	Resistance; fear of facing the truth
I often withdraw from family or friends, not answering calls, not making social plans, etc.	Antisocial issue	Allowed others to steal your energy and feeling depleted with nothing left to give; not wanting one more person to ask something of you or need you
I find myself shutting down around my wife/husband when s/he does not listen or respond to me in a positive, supportive way.	Shutting down issue	Feeling misunderstood or unappreciated as a child; feeling unsafe and a need for protection
I feel strongly one way about something but go against this knowing because of society's or other people's opinions and expectations.	Not being true to self issue	Not trusting intuition; lack of self-confidence
I'm having an affair with a married man/woman.	Lonely and unhappy marriage	No self-love; a disconnect from ourselves, seeking to fill the void with something external

If none of this is clicking with you, or if information and insights still aren't free-flowing, don't despair. Many of you will sit in meditation for an hour and come up empty. Often when we meditate we think nothing is happening because we aren't having any big insights or *Aha!* moments. We come out of meditation without the answers we're looking for, but we feel different somehow and can't explain why. That's because when we're in meditation, our spirit guides are working on our energy, clearing out the old negative thought patterns, and putting us in a higher and more sensitive state of mind for recognizing signs and receiving clarity *after* we've left meditation.

I rarely get the answers I'm looking for during actual meditation. My mind often goes into the process with high hopes for clarity, but then I end up zoning out and coming up blank. This is not a bad thing. In fact, it's the whole point! In meditation, our ambition is to lose our mind control and quiet the inner chitchat so we can sit in stillness. It's usually hours, or even days, after I've been in deep meditation that I suddenly have an epiphany. So, if an hour of quiet meditation only serves to quiet your mind and center your spirit, you're on the right track: You're making space in your mind to receive clarity and the answers will surface in time. Intuitive knowing often strikes when we least expect it—in the grocery store line, sitting in traffic, working out at the gym, in our sleep. The more you commit to doing your favorite meditation, the more you will open up and the easier it will become to feel spiritually connected.

Dream On

If intuitive knowing isn't surfacing in your meditation or in your day-to-day life, you can set the intention and ask for the information to reveal itself through your dreams. Before going to bed, recite your questions and prayers out loud, and if they're written down, place them near your bed or under your pillow.

If the information you need is buried deep in the subconscious, you may be more successful obtaining it while the conscious mind is quieted. Many people have to go to sleep in order for the conscious "outer" mind to relinquish its considerable amount of control over their thoughts. It's when the outer mind sleeps that the inner subconscious mind wakes up, offering clarity and insight through our dreams. Because dreams are often a fantastic mish-mash of imagery and unfamiliar places, I encourage you to record any dream that felt profound and stuck with you throughout the day (even if it didn't make any sense). Write down as many details as you can remember and save it for later. If you're confused about the meaning of a dream, simply ask for further clarity and guidance. I'm always amazed at how often my dreams eventually play out in the physical world.

True Stories: My Stranger Than Fiction Moment

In April 2002, I had a very prophetic dream about my grandfather Harold. It made no sense to me at the time, but it was powerful and felt absolutely real. In the dream, Harold was standing with an angel by his side. He told me it was his time to die, and I was shown that it would be in the month of April. I started crying and he said to me, "You know too much [about the spiritual realm] to be sad. Be happy for me. I get to go home now. And by the way, you need to move to California." *Huh?* I shot straight up in bed, dazed and confused by the intensity and clarity of the dream. My grandpa Harold was eighty-four at the time, suffering from diabetes and Parkinson's disease, but he was lucid and active and getting along pretty well. He didn't seem like a man who was ready to die. And as far as California was concerned—Brian and I were living in

Michigan and had no plans whatsoever to move. The next day, Brian and I went to visit Harold. As soon as I gave him a hug, tears began to stream down my face. The intensity and the "realness" of the dream from the night before washed over me and I felt the sadness of eventually losing him. After a good half hour of small talk, Harold suddenly looked at us and asked, "Did I hear you were planning on moving to California?" Brian and I looked at each other in complete disbelief.

Well, shortly after that visit, I got involved with the entertainment industry and received some loose offers to do a TV show. My manager told me that if I was serious about pursuing work in television, it made sense for me to move to Los Angeles. As I've learned to do over the years, I connected the dots, and in the following months, Brian and I made arrangements to quite literally follow my dream and move to Los Angeles. It took great courage and faith on both of our parts to make such a huge leap based on one weird dream, but I felt strongly that I was receiving divine guidance.

Around that same time, I started having dreams about meeting Tom Hanks (I know, it just keeps getting weirder). In the dreams, I was shaking his hand and he was warmly welcoming me to Los Angeles. I'd wake up every time thinking, *Rebecca, you're really trying to justify this crazy move, aren't you?* Then, weeks later, Brian and I were in Los Angeles looking for a place to live and meeting with a big shot at Sony Studios. On the day of our meeting at Sony, my manager and I arrived early so I could tour the lot. Well, *The Polar Express* was in production at the time, and when my manager scored us access to the set, my jaw dropped when I recognized the lead actor: Tom Hanks. I quickly told my manager about the prophetic dreams I'd been having, and so he dragged me over to Tom Hanks and made an introduction. Tom shook my hand and welcomed me to Los Angeles.

I returned to Michigan convinced that I was on the right path. For whatever reason, Brian and I were meant to move to Los Angeles, and just in case I had any remaining doubts, on April 30, my grandpa Harold passed on into spirit, just as predicted.

✦ TESTIMONIAL

Dear Rebecca . . .

I need to thank you for the reading you did with me today. It was the most extraordinary experience I have ever had. As a therapist, I work deeply and from my heart with my clients. But the gift you bring additionally to your work is the inherent spirituality . . . something which has been a void in my life. You were able to answer some very urgent questions for me . . . and although there is sadness in the knowledge I was looking for, I believe it will allow me to heal and begin to find the peace, which has eluded me for my entire life.

Gratefully,

Jill from Deerfield, Illinois

Step Five: Grieve

Once you're able to name your root issue, you might need to sit with that information for two days, two weeks, or two months. You determine what you need. The important thing is that you don't skip over this next step, the grieving process. It's natural to shy away from grieving in an effort to protect your heart, but grief is necessary for healing. It's imperative that you really face your feelings, acknowledge your grief, and allow yourself to process for however long that takes. Processing that grief will look different from person to person, too. For some, grief may be heartbreak. Others may be mad as hell. It might mean shutting down and going inward. Others will want to talk, talk, talk. Some of us act our grief out physically. I have a client who took up kickboxing as a way to grieve. Another began training for a marathon. As far as I'm concerned, grief is whatever you do to honestly feel what you're feeling.

I often encourage clients to journal their feelings because it worked so well for me. Getting thoughts and emotions down on paper is an effective way to unload and vent. Some people even write a letter to the person who has caused them pain (without the intent of mailing it). Whatever you do, it's important to release all bitterness, anger, and resentment now, so that you don't carry that negative baggage over into the next stage of your life.

I've seen first-hand that everyone's grieving process is unique. Take these two clients for example . . .

True Stories: Grief

Not long ago I did a reading for a woman whose daughter had been murdered a year prior to our session. "My whole family is on my case," my client said. "They tell me it's time to move on, but I'm not ready." I told her, "Well, maybe you're not."

During the reading, her deceased daughter came through and honored her mother's grief. In fact, she gave her mother permission to "grieve in your own time." My client was so thankful for this message and left our session feeling validated and relieved.

In other instances, spirits often nudge their loved ones to let go sooner than later. A client named Michelle once came to me in a deep depression over the death of her mother. She'd been grieving for longer than she could remember. During the reading, her mother immediately came through and told her daughter that it was time to let go— Michelle's grief was only holding both of them back. Neither one of them could spiritually advance while being held in this bubble of grief. This was a hard message for Michelle to hear and she left my office a bit discouraged. This reaction is not uncommon. Many clients feel guilty, as if they're abandoning, or forgetting, the person no longer living. But here's the thing: Letting go of your grief doesn't mean that you're no longer sad—it just means you're ready to move forward. Realize that the dead want us to embrace life! We honor them by allowing their spirit to move on. Letting go is an act of love.

Weeks later, Michelle contacted me. She said her mother visited her in a dream and repeated the same message. Her mother reassured her that they would meet again one day, and that she would always be with her in her heart. In the dream, Michelle realized that her mother was right and that her grief was unhealthy for both of them. With this realization, her mother kissed her cheek and faded away. Michelle said she woke up feeling much lighter and free. "From that moment on," she told me, "a magical thing happened. I stopped feeling sad. My grief is gone."

YOU MAY BE GRIEVING deeply right now over the clarity and insights that you've gained in this chapter. Sit. Take your time. But know that eventually you will have to let your grief go; your intuitive voice will let you know when that time has come. Only when you release the grief will you be able to get present again. And it's in the present moment that you finally get to design and create the life you want for yourself.

◆ TESTIMONIAL

Hi Rebecca,

I saw you for the first time just after my father had committed suicide and I was a mess. I missed my dad terribly, with no release. I felt a tremendous amount of guilt. My father and I had a very disjointed relationship in the last several years of his life. Sitting in your office, I heard my dad coming through. Everything you said hit home. You explained the relationship my father and I had, or the lack thereof. You told me he was sorry. The thought of my dad apologizing and telling me not to let the experiences that I had been through run my life was truly healing.

I loved my dad so dearly and the loss of him had the potential to derail the life I had known. There were so many unanswered questions that were plaguing me. I wandered through the first several months after he died, so disconnected from the world. I was so consumed by grief and guilt that I was unable to function. The messages of love and support have made all of the difference. You telling me that he was taking responsibility not only for his death, but for his lack of participation in my life in the last several years changed me. I had so many issues of rejection and utter lack of love from him before his death that were only magnified after the fact. You were able to be a true messenger for him. You were able to say all of the things he wasn't able to in life . . . and they were so valuable to me.

Thank you, Rebecca, for everything you have done for me.

Amber from Denver, Colorado

Step Six: Forgive

When we hold on to resentment, anger, or bitterness toward another person, a past situation, or toward ourselves, we create negative energy. Carried for an extended period of time, negativity will only create more negativity, which often manifests into physical and emotional ailments. Hate, anger, and resentment commonly lead to disease and depression. The best way to heal an emotional wound is by forgiving. Forgiveness generally comes at the tail end of the grieving process. Forgiveness is powerful. I've seen it positively transform thousands of lives, so naturally, I encourage it!

True Stories: Forgiveness

I once did a reading for a woman whose maternal grandfather came through with an urgent message for his daughter (my client's mother). He passed on to me that she needed to get a mammogram—she had potentially cancerous cells, but if she tended to it right away, she'd be just fine. He went on to express regrets over his abusive behavior when he was alive, and explained that her unresolved pain and anger toward him had manifested in her heart and chest, and without release, it would eventually fester into a cancer that would kill her. He wanted her to understand that he gave her only what he was capable of at the time. He acknowledged that he was flawed and his actions might not be worthy of forgiveness, but now believed that his spirit was. My client agreed to pass along the message to her mother, and the very next day, I got a validating call. Upon hearing the news, her mother had broken down in tears. It turned out that she'd had similar fears about her health and had just had a mammogram. Her doctor had confirmed that she was indeed in the early stages of breast cancer, but she now felt inspired and confident that she would heal.

In a similar reading with a client named Marion, her deceased mother came through with a heartfelt apology for her daughter. Marion's mother was severely depressed, suicidal, and incapable of caring for Marion when she was a young girl. As a result, Marion took on the caretaker role and parented herself. Her mother explained that she was coming through to help heal the pain that Marion had been carrying with her from childhood. At the time of the reading, Marion was suffering from chronic fatigue syndrome, low self-esteem, and low self-love. In fact, she was going down a very similar path that her mother had traveled in life. To put a halt to the negative cycle of loneliness, resentment, and fear, Marion's mother encouraged her daughter to focus on her photography and artistic expression, one of the few things that gave Marion strength and joy. But here's the most important part: By giving her mother permission to step in and guide her, Marion finally forgave her. And Marion's act of forgiveness allowed her to take back her own power and move on.

When we forgive, we rid ourselves of stagnant, negative energy and allow room for new positive energy to move in. Are you ready to forgive the person who played a part in your issue? If this feels hard to do without guidance, try the following meditation.

MEDITATION

Release the Grief and Forgive

What you'll need: A candle and a match. A place to sit quietly.

Close your eyes and do your simple breathing meditation. Take several deep inhales and exhales and get present. After a few minutes, open your eyes and light your candle while affirming:

> I am letting go of all pain, suffering, and despair I experienced in the past from (this person, situation, my own creation). I surrender it to God's hands.

Close your eyes once again and mentally invite your spirit guides to help you release any pain you're holding onto. Ask them to help you forgive. Imagine your spirit guides taking your hurt feelings into the light for healing and transformation.

Breathe. Allow your mind to be still and quiet . . . seeing, hearing, or feeling nothing but the stillness. Just be. Sit in this space of lightness, forgiveness, and love for as long as feels right for you. When you're ready to let forgiveness replace your old feelings of pain, blow out the candle, and release your grief to the Universe.

◆ TESTIMONIAL

Dear Rebecca,

I never thought I would be happy again after the loss of my sister. I had been struggling with the loss because she was my best friend. My spirit guides must have been helping me the day I flipped the TV to the Rachael Ray Show *and saw you helping a lady connect with her mother. I got on the Internet and found your Web site. I thank God for the Internet. I was put on your list and waited for you to call because I needed to connect with my sister in a BIG way. She is a good soul and didn't tell anyone she was sick and I now understand why. She lived in Florida and I didn't see her at the end, otherwise I would have known she was dying. When you called, all you said was, "Pray that your loved ones come through and say your name." You immediately brought through my grandmother, a huge force for good in my childhood who guided me through the ordeals of an abusive father who I am truly blessed to have survived. You said they were allowing him to come through, but that he was paying for what he did. The only justice was that he came through first to apologize and that he couldn't hurt me anymore. You said that my mother needed to forgive him. I helped her with this. She said forgiving him lifted a weight off her shoulders. She says she feels joy now. You said my grandmother was a spirit guide for me and that she had been worried for me the last eighteen months. This was exactly how long my sister had been gone. The entire conversation with you was an Aha! moment. You asked if I was a nurse and I knew where you were*

going with that also. I always put others before myself because I never thought I should come first. My father would say I was never good enough regardless of my accomplishments. You told me to stop thinking like that and start living my life. That was a big message for me. I feel everything will be all right now. I thank God for you, Rebecca.
  Sincerely,
  Susan from Severn, Maryland

Forgiving Yourself

Now can you take responsibility for the role *you* played in your health, career, money, relationship, or addiction issue? Is it possible that you attracted the current situation through your own thoughts and actions?

Again, this doesn't mean you're at fault or to blame. I want you to get away from blaming others and particularly yourself. Blame does not serve you. It's wasted energy that holds you back. It keeps you in a victimized state of mind and no matter how much you want to point the finger it will never change the past. Taking responsibility is about acknowledging your choices and not blaming. We *always* have the power to choose how we respond to a situation. (As I've said before, it's not what happens to us, but how we react to or handle it that matters most!) Once we forgive our contribution to the struggle that has been holding us back, the Universe provides us with the opportunity to re-do. New situations will come along where we can make better choices for ourselves and break the cycle of negativity.

True Stories: Forgive Yourself

I once worked with a client who grew up with a very narcissistic mother. Because he felt ignored and desperately wanted his mother's love and attention, he indulged her self-centered behavior and stifled his own needs. As an adult, he married a woman who also demanded the spotlight and leaned on him to boost her ego. As the years went by, his intolerance for needy behavior grew. He resented his kids, his employees, and anyone who *needed* him. Guess what happened next? He continued to attract people into his life who drained his energy. In my session with him, his grandfather came through and helped him connect his anger and resentment back to the root cause—his narcissistic mother. His grandfather encouraged him to stop blaming and start forgiving his mother and himself. You see, my client's *response* to his mother's behavior was *his* piece to own. He alone made the choice to stifle his needs, invite people into his life who needed him, and then resent them for it afterward. Once he recognized and took responsibility for his contribution to the situation, he regained power over his life and started making different choices.

WHEN THINKING ABOUT what choices you have made in reaction to your root issue, try saying, *I ask for help in forgiving myself for poor choices I have made that have hurt others and myself. I ask that Spirit cleanse me of all guilt, resentment, or negative energy that I may be holding on to in connection to this. I am willing to find the lesson in this situation and choose to grow from it.*

✦ TESTIMONIAL

Dear Rebecca,

My baby boys were born prematurely and did not survive long. My first twin boy, Jonathan, was born alive and my second twin boy, James, was stillborn. Because Jonathan was so little his lungs weren't fully developed. The doctors said that he was too small to try to resuscitate and that babies that small would not live despite life-sustaining efforts. They told me that all I could do was hold him and make him comfortable. I had to sit and hold my son while he suffocated. His tiny body could not produce oxygen. It was the longest thirty minutes of my life.

After Jonathan passed I was unable to get rid of the guilt. Was there some way that I could have kept him in my body another two weeks? Could he have been helped more by the doctors? I only imagined that his death must have been horrible and he was too small to express his discomfort or pain. Moms are supposed to protect their children and all I could do was sit and watch him die. I could not quit thinking that I could have done more to make his passing easier.

During my reading in July 2008, my baby boy, Jonathan, came through and told me that his death was not as bad as it looked. He said that he was not in pain. It wasn't the horrible death that I had always thought that it was. I am finally forgiving myself and I don't have the sick feeling in my stomach that I used to have when I remember his passing. My reading with you has allowed me to let go of my guilt! A huge burden has been lifted off of my shoulders. I still miss my baby boys and I still mourn their deaths. I think about them and talk to them every day. You never get over the death of a child, no matter what their age. But I have forgiven myself and that makes life better. Thanks, Rebecca, for being good at what you do and for bringing my boys through.

Tori from Houston, Texas

Step Seven: Find the Gifts

Now that you've gotten some of the gunk out of your system and practiced forgiveness, I want you to focus on finding the gifts from your struggle—come on, there's always at least one—and see how they have allowed you to grow.

If you've discovered, for instance, that you're unorganized and scattered due to childhood verbal abuse, can you find the gift in this? *A gift? Where's the gift in that?* Admittedly, the gift isn't always easy to spot, but trust me—there's one in there somewhere. I've met clients who became pros at conflict resolution as a result of the verbal abuse they suffered as kids. When we choose to acknowledge the lesson within our personal challenge, we take back our power and stop being a victim. Every hardship offers us an opportunity to spiritually grow if we allow it to.

AFFIRMATION

I choose to see everything as a gift.

True Stories: Gifts

For years, I read a client named Jan, and every year, her weight issues would come up. She always had the same complaint—she couldn't lose the last fifty pounds. She was perpetually miserable about her weight and I really felt for her. After all, I'd been there.

Last year, she came to see me more discouraged than ever. In addition to her ongoing battle with weight, she'd lost her job. She added unemployment stress to her "my life sucks" list and admitted that she didn't know what to do. I encouraged her to take a little time and let her intuition lead her down a new career path. She called me soon afterward. Intuition had whispered in her ear! She remembered that she'd always wanted to be a massage therapist. Almost as soon as she "named" her forgotten dream out loud, an opportunity opened up for her and that's when her life turned around. She began training to become a massage therapist and, in doing so, she began to lose her extra weight.

A MARRIED COUPLE once came to me while they were grieving the loss of their oldest daughter. She'd died from brain cancer at age eleven. Before her illness, the husband had struggled with his belief in God. He was very cynical in nature and closed off emotionally. When his daughter got sick, she remained optimistic and became a spiritual teacher to her family. She told them that she was going to die, but that it was "all okay" because this was her purpose—to spiritually open her family's minds and hearts. Her death and subsequent presence during their reading with me served to convert him from a cynic to a complete believer in the afterlife and renewed his faith in God.

EXERCISE

Three Gifts

The intention of this next exercise is to help you find the gifts, or opportunities for growth, from your struggle. Instead of feeling weakened by circumstances from your past, try transforming them into a source of strength and wisdom. On the lines below, list a troubling situation in your past (job layoff, divorce, death of a loved one) and the unexpected opening it provided for you. Need some help getting started? Answer the following:

What exactly was my situation?

_____

Was it my own creation or totally out of my control?

_____

Was I expecting this to happen (on an unconscious or intuitive level) or did it come as a complete surprise?

_____

How had I been feeling prior to the "change"?

_____

How am I feeling now?

_____

Did this situation serve as a "wake up call" to my life?

_____

Now ask yourself some bigger picture questions: What has this experience taught me and how has it helped me to grow? How has it helped me become who I am today? When we take time to notice and focus on the gifts, we attract more good things into our life experience.

For example, a client of mine lost her job. For weeks she searched for a new one, but none of the positions she applied for worked out. Finding the gift in her situation was the last thing on her mind—she was in a state of panic thinking, *How am I going to pay my bills?* During the time she was unemployed, she spent more time with her kids and husband. After a couple months, she landed a job in a field totally different from where she was before (and this gig was more fulfilling and paid her better!). In hindsight, my client was able to see that losing her job offered her an opportunity to switch careers and bond with her family.

On the lines below, list three gifts from your troubling situation.

_____

_____

_____

_____

_____

_____

_____

_____

_____

_____

_____

_____

Coming up blank? No problem. Your emotions may still be too charged or raw. Give it time. Be patient and trust that eventually you'll be able to see the grand plan at work. For now, you've planted the seed in your mind to start thinking about your struggle in a different way. Before we move on to the next step, I want to share my own "diamond in the rough" experience with you.

My Diamond in the Rough

A few years ago, my father died. His death was tragic and sudden and I'll share the full story with you in Chapter Six: Do the Work. Not long after Dad's death, I got pregnant. Twelve weeks later, I miscarried. Three months later, I got pregnant again and miscarried a second time.

I was devastated, angry, and heartbroken. I'd had enough death! I demanded to know: *God, why is this happening to me?*

After grieving for what felt like a very long time, I recognized that my miscarriages offered me an opportunity to grow. (To be clear, I didn't get there right away. It took months of sitting with it to start seeing the situation clearly.) Big surprise here: Meditation helped me connect the dots. It allowed my suppressed feelings over losing someone significant to rise the surface. I was able to work out these unresolved issues in therapy and later came to understand that making peace with my father's death was important work for me to do before I brought another child into the world. Additionally, the miscarriages made me even more grateful for the child I already had. My son Jakob was healthy and beautiful, and when my second son finally came along, Jakob was ready and mature enough to take on the big brother role for Sam. Lastly, my experience gave me a deeper level of understanding and compassion for clients who have lost someone dear to them. After personally losing my dad and later accepting his untimely death, I could offer my clients reassurance that everything happens for a reason and to trust in divine timing.

Step Eight: Let Go

Letting go brings you full circle. That's what it's done for me. I'm living proof that it works! That said, I know it can be difficult to see the big picture and accept that your life is unfolding in perfect order. So, don't beat yourself up if you're not quite there yet. You began your work in this chapter by setting the intention to be centered in a space of pure love and positive energy. Then you asked Spirit to help guide you toward clarity. You sat with your grief and forgave. Now the only thing left to do is to relinquish control and trust that what you need is on the way. By letting go, we release our need to affect outcomes, which stalls or slows down the process of receiving. By letting go, we are placing our trust in

God, Source, Universe. That doesn't mean you're totally off the hook and you get to sit back and do nothing. It's not a letting go of responsibility or effort. You still have your own work to do and we'll get to that in Chapter Six: Do the Work.

EXERCISE

Letting Go

As an exercise for letting go, I like to literally place it in God's hands. Almost every morning after reciting my prayers, intentions, and gratitude for everything and everyone in my life, I imagine God's hands cupped and outstretched before me and I hand a bright, magnetic ball of light, which represents my life, over and into those hands. This mental transfer of power (remember: we can't control it all) symbolizes my trust and belief that my life is in good hands.

One of my best friends, Elizabeth Picone, likes to do a balloon exercise. She takes a Sharpie marker and writes on a helium balloon all the things weighing her down. Once she's got all her worries, fears, and concerns written on the balloon, she says a prayer and lets it go, watching her anxieties float away.

GET PRESENT

When we're able to shake off the mistakes, regrets, and confinements from our past, we begin to live more joyfully in the present. And when we're living in the present, we can intentionally create the life we want. So, are you ready to get present? I hope so, because I'm going to let you in on a little secret—there is *only* the present. Everything else is an illusion. Things in the past *happened* and things in the future *will happen*, but they aren't happening NOW. *Am I right?* Many of us spend the bulk of our energy and time drifting between memories of the past and projections of the future, none of which is as relevant as what's happening right now. What if I told you that "heaven" was not a place, but a state of mind where we're simply living peacefully in the moment? Would that change how you lived your life now? As Rabbi Elli Kaplan Spitz wrote in his book *Does the Soul Survive?*, "Our past has meaning and our future has relevance only if we live with awareness and compassion in the present moment."

Being present means fully embracing the right here, right now. When we stay focused on the now, our lives will unfold in perfect time.

Hold On! I Don't Get It: I understand that obsessing about the future isn't healthy or productive, but surely we have to think about it! We can't just go through life without making plans, right?

Here's the Deal: Yes, you have to be able to look ahead and plan for things like weddings, vacations, and saving for your kids' college educations. And you have to make dinner reservations and doctor appointments, and schedule meetings. There are many things—big and small—that we have to plan for, but scheduling events is very different from fixating and trying to control future outcomes one minute at a time. After we take aggressive steps to put our dreams (financial freedom, finding our soul mate, career change, release from illness) into motion, we can relax in the present knowing that experiences will play out the way they need to for us to learn and grow. One of my favorite sayings is, "Man plans and God laughs," and it's really true. So, plan the best you can and then put it in God's hands, surrendering any attachment to the outcome. Think you can do this? I won't lie—relinquishing control takes some getting used to.

What This Means for You: It is in the present that we are most power-ful and have the clearest connection to intuitive and spiritual awareness. The only way I'm able to successfully connect with Spirit in readings is by being totally present. I get in my zone. I don't think about what hap-pened yesterday or what's going to happen later tonight. In fact, I try not to think at all!

Once we're able to identify the root of why we're stuck, we're ready to ask for spiritual support and guidance as we move forward with our lives. In Chapter Five: Tap the Source, I'll show you how to do just that.

5

✳

Tap the Source

Now for the part you've been waiting for! For the past couple of chapters, you've been working hard to develop your intuition. (Give yourself a pat on the back. You deserve it!) Our intuition connects us to spirit energy that we can't see, but exists all the same. Spirit guidance is available to us as soon as we ask for it, and once we know how to tap into it, Spirit will begin to deliver us powerful messages.

Like many in my line of work, I use the word *signs* to describe how Spirit communicates with us. (I tried coming up with something more original and clever, but always came back to "signs.") Especially when we're faced with challenging times, feeling hopeless and lost, these signs offer proof that there's a plan at work around us and that we're on the right path.

In this chapter, you'll begin to communicate with Spirit on your own. That's right, on your own! I'll explain how to:

- Ask spirit energy for help and guidance,
- Understand how spirits "talk" to you,
- Prepare yourself to listen, and
- Know what to listen for.

If you've gotten this far into the book, it's because you're curious about what kind of insight spirit energy has for you, so let's first talk about how to go about asking for it.

As I mentioned earlier, spirits won't barge in and offer you guidance unless you ask them to. You have to *invite* Spirit in. (They're polite that way.) Without permission, they won't tell you much—beyond popping in and saying "Hi," they'll keep their opinions to themselves.

> **AFFIRMATION**
>
> *I am open to receiving spirit guidance.*

Should you want their guidance (and I'm guessing you do), the good news is that your invitation needn't be complicated. Spirit energy doesn't require a formal request. Just like with meditation, you can be sitting in your office, in your car, or in your pajamas on your living-room couch, and simply say, "Hey, I need some help here!" Personally, I walk around my house talking to Spirit like I'm gabbing with one of my best girlfriends, but that's just me.

The key to asking effectively is putting your heart into your request. You have to *mean* it. *Spirits pick up on our thoughts and feelings, so if you fake it they'll know it.* Then, once you've whole-heartedly invited Spirit in, you need to be open to receiving the information that comes through. Keep in mind that spirits have their own agenda (not in a scary, controlling way, just that sometimes they know better what we need than we do), so they may not cover the issues that *you* feel are the most important. I always suggest to clients to surrender any expectations they may have and trust that they will receive the guidance that will help them most—and that's really what we all want, isn't it?

The second thing is to be patient. Like it is with quieting your mind, recognizing and interpreting spirit energy takes practice. Plus, how clearly spirits communicate depends on how well they communicated in life, and how evolved they are. Expect a certain level of frustration and self-doubt in the beginning.

MENTAL TUNE-UP

So, asking for help is the first thing, but knowing how to then intercept that help from the spirits that surround us all the time is another thing altogether. Like radio waves, spiritual information is constantly being broadcast around us, so it's really just a matter of learning how to tune into it. It's like turning on the radio—if we want to hear classical music, we have to turn the dial to the classical station. Get it?

To interpret what Spirit is broadcasting you'll be using your five senses just like you do in your day-to-day life. And just as you may feel that some of your senses are more reliable than others for making every-day judgments, you have senses, or *Clairs,* that are stronger for hearing spirit.

Sense of Style

Let's pick up where we left off in Chapter Two: A Different Kind of Self-Help and figure out what *your* dominant Clairs are. First, here's a quick summary:

MANY OF US ARE highly visual and able to understand an idea best when we see it written or sketched out as an image, on a computer screen, on television, or on a canvas. Visual people often choose to be art-ists, builders, photographers, and designers. If this sounds familiar, you may have a clear sense of seeing called *clairvoyance.*

For others, we may best retain and comprehend information when we *hear* it spoken aloud. Our natural talents tend to lie in our auditory faculties, often making us gifted musicians, singers, writers, and public

Take Out the Trash

For all the exercises that follow, I want to stress the importance of clearing your mind. (I know, I'm a nag.) Think of the doubting, distracting, and negative chitchat in your head as *mind garbage*. Until you take out the trash, so to speak, you won't be able to connect intuitively or with Spirit. So, do yourself a favor and spend some time in meditation before attempting to plug in.

speakers. If this feels right to you, you may have a clear sense of hearing called *clairaudience*.

Some of us are highly sensitive and are in tune with not only our own feelings, but also the feelings of others. This makes us natural healers and caregivers, inspiring us to pursue careers as doctors, therapists, counselors, and teachers. If this is you, you may have a clear sense of feeling called *clairsentience*.

And then there are those of us who were born with a strong connection to our intuitive voice. We seem to just *know* the facts without being tipped off by anyone or anything particular—we feel things deep in our bones with a sense of certainty. Philosophers, professors, doctors, scientists, and powerful sales and business leaders tend to be highly intuitive. These folks may have a clear sense of knowing called *claircognizance*.

Most of us have one or two dominant senses for both our physical and spiritual bodies (so don't worry if you can't decide between two of the above), and understanding which will be most reliable to us will make sensing Spirit a lot less frustrating.

EXERCISE

Find Your Sense of Style or Style of Sense

Now how do you recognize what your preferred or dominant style of sensing is? Begin by sitting in a comfortable place where you won't be distracted for a few minutes. Scan the area around you, taking in all details and feelings of where you are. Then close your eyes and focus on your breath. Breathe deeply and slowly as you mentally review what caught your attention when you scanned the room. Was it the *sight* of something that stood out, the *sound* of something that you heard, the *feeling* of something registering in your stomach or heart, or a strong *thought* about something that hit you from out of the blue?

Still not sure what your dominant Clair is? No problem. Try the next exercise.

EXERCISE

Word Search

For this exercise, as you read through the list that follows, write down your first impression for each word. What do you immediately see, hear, feel, know, smell?

1) Fire

_____

2) Florida

_____

3) High school

_____

4) Money

_____

5) Suicide

_____

6) Pizza

_____

7) Autumn

_____

8) Dog

_____

9) Skiing

_____

10) Ocean

_____

11) Mother

_____

12) Airplane

_____

To give you an example of how one word can elicit a range of responses, consider the word *ocean*. Someone might *see* the color blue (clear seeing). Another might *hear* the sound of waves crashing (clear hearing). And another might *feel* the warmth of the sun on his or her face (clear feeling).

After you've noted your initial impressions, take a deeper look at what you wrote down. For example, if *money* triggered the word *shopping*, ask yourself, did I *see* myself shopping at the mall (clear seeing)? Did I imagine how it *felt* to be in a crowded mall or how wonderful it *feels* to buy new things (clear feeling)? Did I *hear* a bunch of loud chatter around me (clear hearing)?

After you have a better idea of what your strongest sense is, follow up with the next series of exercises. Each will help you better understand and sharpen your particular style of sensing. Begin by trying the exercise that correlates with the sense you believe is most dominant for you, and then try the other ones as well. Spirit will try to communicate with you through your strongest sense, but if you're not getting the message, Spirit will try another way, so it's not a bad idea to develop all four. That way, you won't miss the call.

EXERCISE FOR CLEAR SEEING

Are You Seeing Clearly?

For this exercise, put a specific object or picture a few feet in front of you and study it. Then close your eyes and focus on the space in between your eyebrows, otherwise known as your "third eye." Breathe slowly and deeply for several minutes to quiet your mind. Once you feel relaxed, open your eyes and focus on the object for a few more minutes. Then close your eyes again and focus on your third eye. Visualize the object; really focus on the small details of what it looks like. The easier it is for you to focus and the clearer the detail, the more open and active your seeing sense, or *clairvoyance*, is. Repeat this exercise whenever you have an extra moment to strengthen your vision and become familiar with what spirit information looks like.

EXERCISE FOR CLEAR HEARING

Did You Hear That Right?

Similar to automatic writing, this exercise allows Spirit to send you messages that do not present themselves as images. To begin, get a pen and paper, or turn on your computer and open a new document so that you can type freely. Hold the pen in your hand lightly or gently place your hands on the keyboard in front of you. Ask: "What do you want me to know at this time?" The words will either come from inside or outside your mind; you may hear a faint inner voice along with a strong desire to write. Don't hear or feel anything? Don't give up. Just begin writing whatever thoughts or feelings come to you to start the flow of energy. Eventually Spirit will come through and the writing will pick up in intensity, speed, and clarity. You may feel light pressure around your head, light-headedness, or dizziness—this is nothing to worry about. These side effects usually dissipate with time as you become more attuned to hearing spirit energy.

EXERCISE FOR CLEAR FEELING

Do Ya Feel It?

This exercise requires a partner and a special possession of hers for you to hold. Ask for anything she uses on a daily basis, such as car keys, rings, watches, eyeglasses, or wallets. Hold the item in your non-dominant hand. (For example, if you are right-handed, hold the item in your left hand for the duration of the exercise. While your left hand may be less useful for writing, the less dominant hand is the one that allows you to receive information most clearly.) Sit facing your partner, with both of you closing your eyes and focusing on the item. Mentally ask Spirit what you should know about the item and the person it belongs to. Once you start receiving impressions, whether it is a thought, feeling, vision, or word, simply speak it aloud to your partner. Do not edit, censor, or interpret the information. Keep your logical mind out of this exercise as much as you can. The key is to allow room for your intuition to answer the question you asked. You'll be amazed at how much information makes sense to your partner, even if it holds no meaning for you. Just trust and relax, and notice how you get better each time you try this.

EXERCISE FOR CLEAR KNOWING

How Did You Know?

This exercise requires you to carry around a small notebook or voice recorder. For a period of a week, tell yourself—out loud, if you want—that you are open and willing to receive any guidance and insight in the form of clear knowing: ideas, hunches, and personal observations that come to you as you go about your day. Then use your notebook or recorder to record all thoughts or ideas that pop into your mind from out of the blue. It may be something about yourself, a family member or a close friend, or an unrelated event. Don't let your mind start to engage in interpreting, exaggerating, or judging the thought or idea. Just record it exactly as it came in and let it be. Time will be your "proof" when you find that an idea you had a week ago suddenly turns out to be true. That's when you go back to your recorded information and confirm that you had prior knowing of the event before it physically played out.

Hold On! I Don't Get It: I understand the idea of quieting my mind and tuning in to my dominant senses, but then what? What am I waiting for?

Here's the Deal: In the beginning, making yourself open to Spirit may feel awkward or like it's not working, but stick with it.

What This Means for You: When your intuitive brain finally snaps into place, here's an idea of what you can expect:

What Happens When We See?

As I explained in Chapter Two: A Different Kind of Self-Help, intuitive seeing typically comes when visual impressions of the past, present, or future flash through our minds—sort of like a daydream. These images can be subtle and come through just briefly, so you must have a quieted and present mind in order to pick them up in the first place. They also come in clips and phrases, so it's up to you to correctly piece together the information to accurately interpret what spirit energy is trying to communicate.

What Happens When We Hear?

Intuitive hearing generally comes as words, sounds, or music in your head, and sometimes—although this is unusual—out loud outside of your head. Imagine hanging up the phone after gabbing with your girlfriend and replaying parts of the conversation in your mind. Most likely you will "hear" your voice and the voice of your friend, right? Your mind is re-creating the actual dialogue that took place. This is how I hear Spirit. On rare occasions, Spirit will find a way to create audible sounds and words to get our attention, too. In this case, we often have to fill in the gaps to understand the meaning. For example, I might hear a sound like "J-N" and then ask my client, "Who is John, Joan, Jen, etc.?"

What Happens When We Feel?

Many of us have a strong sense of feeling without even being aware of it. Helen Keller said: "The best and most beautiful things in the world cannot be seen or even touched. They must be felt with the heart." Though we all have the ability to feel our own emotions, many women also have the ability to empathically feel the emotions of other people and spirit energies around them. Have you ever gotten a strong feeling about someone you just met—positive or negative—and then felt the "chills" for no apparent reason? If this sounds familiar, then you've already sensed energy. Some people call this trusting your first impression. This initial feeling, or gut reaction, most often tells you the truth. Learn to trust what you feel. In my work, I often experience sympathetic pain associated with someone who has passed. I may feel a strong pinch in my chest, indicating a heart attack, or a cramping sensation in my stomach, indicating a major stomach issue. This probably won't happen to you, so don't freak out. I just mention it as an extreme example of clear feeling.

> AFFIRMATION
>
> *I am aware of spirit energy around me.*

What Happens When We Know?

Have you ever had a strong sense of knowing something without understanding why? It's like . . . you just *know*. This is spirit energy impressing you with insights. Because they seem to come from out of nowhere, intuitive knowing requires a tremendous amount of trust on your part. It's much easier to dismiss these thoughts when your logical mind immediately asks, *How do you know that? Why would you think that? Where's the evidence?* The next time you experience a strong, clear sense of knowing, try to keep your overworked, logical mind out of it. Instead of second-guessing yourself, go with the feeling and see what happens. My bet is that within a short amount of time you will be validated by some event or person who confirms your "hunch." That's when you can tell your logical mind, *HA! I told you so!*

GET CLEAR

Now that you know the different ways that Spirit can speak to you, I urge you to rethink how you pay attention throughout your day. Spirit is constantly tapping us on the shoulder . . . *tap, tap, tap* . . . but many of us lose out on this powerful guidance because we're lingering in the past—obsessing about a guy or a lost opportunity—or racing toward the future—planning our week or what we'll do when we finally get back into our skinny jeans. To hear Spirit, we need to stop, park it in the present, and take a look around. When you do this, you'll start to recognize messages everywhere—too many "coincidences" that can't be waved off.

Speaking of, a few years ago I decided to replace the word *coincidence* with *synchronicity* in my vocabulary. Why? *Coincidence* implies chance, while *synchronicity* is how life is intended to play out. When we are in sync, in the present, and open, synchronicities are abundant—they become part of our everyday routine. And Spirit loves to point them out. If this sounds amazing—it is! I still laugh out loud when events line up. Or sometimes I break down in tears. It's humbling, even after ten years of doing this work.

True Stories: Synchronicity

A while ago, my husband, Brian, dragged me to go shopping for carpet and tile for our basement. FYI: This is the type of errand I dread because

I can never make up my mind about this kind of stuff. During the drive to the store, I silently asked Spirit to make this quick, simple, and painless (yes, I'm constantly pulling in favors). As soon as we got there, I looked at my watch and it said 12:14 (my dad's birthday). I smiled to myself because Dad used to tease me when he was alive about how much house-y tasks annoy me. We got out of the car just as a truck drove by with SHALOM ("Hello" in Hebrew) written in huge letters on its side. I inwardly asked, "Dad, are you here running this errand with us?" We walked into the store and the carpet guy had more than five thousand carpet samples to choose from. As anticipated, I was overwhelmed and asked him what he suggested. He pulled out two dozen swatches and my eye instantly went to one of them. I pointed at it and said to Brian, "That's it!" Carpet guy turned over the swatch and read the color— "PEANUT SHELL." I gasped. My dad called me "peanut" my whole life and his name is Shelly. Suffice it to say, we went with Peanut Shell.

Hold On! I Don't Get It: Why do spirits care about mundane things like carpet colors?

Here's the Deal: They don't. But they bring them up for a couple of reasons. During readings, I insist that spirits mention trivial things about my clients' lives that I would have no way of knowing. That way, when Spirit brings up the bathroom you just painted green yesterday or the significance of the necklace you're wearing, you're more apt to trust that Spirit is truly present. Once you feel certain that I've made a genuine connection for you, then spirits can pass on the more important messages—*I love you. I'm sorry. It's time to move on with your life, etc.*

What This Means for You: Outside of a reading, when we're running around doing our day-to-day stuff, distracted and not picking up on psychic energy, Spirit will find silly ways to get our attention (e.g., the Peanut Shell carpet color) to make their presence known. Most often, they just want to say hello and remind us that we're not alone and that they're still alive in spirit and in a good place.

SOMETIMES SPIRIT WILL provide guidance by confirming our own resourcefulness and knowing. For example, during my last pregnancy I put on some extra weight. Okay, *a lot* of extra weight, and I knew it was because I wasn't taking very good care of myself. I was working hard, not sleeping enough, and eating badly, but I made excuses—telling myself that all the extra weight was baby weight. *Pass the potatoes!* Well, when I went in for a routine doctor's appointment and got on the scale, my doc said, "Whoa. You've put on a lot of weight very quickly. Is everything okay? Do we need to talk about your diet?" *Uh-oh. Busted.*

I was embarrassed and disappointed with myself—she was only telling me what I already knew, but was ignoring. I left the doctor's office knowing that I had better shape up—and right away. Once back in my car, I called Brian and said, "My doctor just busted me for eating too much."

"You're in trouble!" Brian teased.

"Ha, ha," I said. "It's all that New York pizza we've been eating." And right then, a car with a "NY PIZZA" vanity license plate drove right past me! This was Spirit's way of saying, *Yes, your intuitive knowing is right. Start taking better care of yourself. No more pizza!*

ANGELS, SPIRIT GUIDES, AND GHOSTS—*OH MY!*

Before we go any deeper into Spirit communication, I want to spend some time talking about *who* might answer your call. Spirit is a broad term. Up to this point, I've included your passed loved ones and spirit guides under this umbrella, but now I want to explain that it doesn't stop there.

When I do readings, I mentally see, or tune into, several layers of spirit energy above my clients' heads. Think of these layers as a rainbow expanding from the inside out, climbing higher and higher.

The first layer—and the one closest to us—is the energy of deceased loved ones, relatives, and friends. This is the energy I work with most. Most often, our passed loved ones connect with us simply to say hello and remind us that they're still with us. Sometimes they have valuable guidance for us, but because we don't suddenly become all knowing and God-like when we pass into the spirit world, we have to take what they say with a grain of salt. Your aunt Suzy is still Aunt Suzy! Just because she is now free of her body and ego doesn't mean she knows everything about you and your life. She does have 20/20 hindsight, which is an advantage, but she doesn't hold the keys to the Universe. So, when you hear from Spirit, ask your intuition, *Does this feel loving, does this feel right?* Most often, your passed loved ones will have no agenda other than to offer you tenderness and loving insight. But keep this important thing in mind: If your brother wasn't trustworthy in life, he's not necessarily going to be any different in Spirit.

Spirit Guides

The spirits who *always* have our best interests in mind and have the ability to see our past, present, and future are our spirit guides. Their energy occupies the second layer of the rainbow. They point us in the right direction, comfort us in times of need, and warn us off from danger. They're loving beings who once lived in a physical body and who, in spirit form, are put on assignment with us (*who* assigns them? Hold on—that's coming up next). Over the course of our lives, we may have several spirit guides who come and go as needed. Their purpose is to help us learn and grow, while balancing out their own negative mojo. Sometimes our spirit guides will give a passed loved one (like Aunt Suzy) a deeper peek at our lives if they feel that providing them with certain details and information will help *them* help *us*. My grandmother Babe was not only a deceased relative, but also on assignment with me as a spirit guide. I needed her help to move forward in my life, and she needed to move me forward to neutralize her own suicide. In other words, she rubbed my back and I rubbed hers. But again, our spirit guides won't interfere in our lives unless or until we ask them to. They're waiting to help us, but we have to ask for it!

Guardian Angels

Our spirit guides come and go, but our guardian angels are with us for life. Everyone has at least one or two of these super helpers from the moment we're born, and their energy occupies the next tier up in the rainbow. *Do they have wings?* (I know you're thinking this.) Angels are actually just beings of light, but they sometimes appear to us in the form we need in order to believe in their existence. Early on in my mediumship, I woke up in the middle of the night to find a faceless woman standing at the end of my bed. Now if that won't make you a believer, I don't know what will! Well, I recognized that her presence was loving and good, so I didn't totally freak out. She stood there for about five seconds and then faded away. I later read in one of my many paranormal books that a faceless energy is angelic. It was the first and last time she appeared: She came through just that one time to let me know she was there and that's all it took—I was sold!

Angels respond to our calls for guidance, assistance, protection, and comfort. If we are attuned to them, we can feel their loving presence. When we feel a wave of love, comfort, and peace swell up inside us, we have our angels to thank for it. Sometimes the subtle presence of an angel will give me the chills—the good kind.

Most people go through life unaware of this guidance, although it's available to us as soon as we choose to acknowledge it. On a soul level, we know angels are with us (just ask any child if they believe in angels), but our adult minds have forgotten them—we need to *lose our mind*, so to speak, or tap into our spiritual senses to re-remember their presence.

Angels primarily work on the emotional plane, tending to our spiritual and emotional needs. In other words, they aren't the ones who will offer you career advice. And to answer an earlier question, it is our guardian angels who assign spirit guides based on their history and if they can empathize with the lessons we need to learn. If a spirit agrees to do the work, it's an opportunity to evolve without having to reincarnate back into a body.

> **AFFIRMATION**
>
> I am open to receiving help from my guides and angels.

Many people loosely refer to the term *guardian angel* as any spirit who is "watching over us." And while many of our passed loved ones do watch over us, they can't *technically* be our guardian angel because our angels are with us from birth until death.

As with spirits and our guides, we must ask our guardian angels for their help and give them permission to play a role in our lives. The only exception of "angelic intervention" is when we're put in a life-threatening situation and it's just not our time to go. Our guardian angels exist to keep us on the right path and out of harm's way.

Ghosts and Lost Souls

As I mentioned earlier, I don't work with ghosts or lost souls (or rather, they don't choose to work with me!). I work with spirits who are at peace and who are simply coming through to reconnect with their loved ones.

Earthbound ghosts and lost souls are spirits who are still clinging to their physical lives, reluctant to move on. (What can I say—they were comfortable in their skin.) There are a variety of reasons why these spirits don't want to let go and why they're in limbo land. Some feel confused

Calling for Backup

In the book *Angels Watching Over Me*, author Betty Malz tells a story about a young woman who was walking home from work in Brooklyn one night and had to go past a creepy guy loitering against a building. She was fearful. There had been muggings in the area recently, and she prayed for protection from the Archangel Michael and from her spirit guides. Although she could feel creepy guy watching her as she walked by, he didn't move. A short time after she got home, she heard sirens and saw police lights. The next day her neighbor told her someone had been raped, in the same place she had seen the suspicious guy!

She wondered if the man she saw was the rapist, because if he were, she could identify him. She called the police and discovered they had a suspect in custody. Sure enough, she identified him in the lineup and wondered, *Why didn't he attack me? I was just as vulnerable as the next woman who came along.* The policeman later asked the rapist if he remembered another young woman who passed by him that evening. He said, "I remember her. But why would I have bothered her? She was walking down the street with two big guys, one on either side of her."

about how they died and need answers or want to make amends with the living before they move on. Some formed such strong attachments to their home, business, or family that they can't fathom releasing any of it. Other spirits are afraid of judgment from God for poor choices they made in life, and some spirits are simply unaware that they are dead (yes, just like Bruce Willis's character in *The Sixth Sense*). When these spirits come through, their presence is typically anxious, angry, sad, and sometimes confused, though they're generally not evil or harmful—they're just lost souls in need of direction.

Hold On! I Don't Get It: But you said that you work with spirits with unresolved issues or who want to make amends. How are they any different from the ghosts you've just described?

Here's the Deal: Society tends to throw around the word *ghost* loosely. I should clarify that a ghost is simply energy, not evil or dark, just an apparitionlike form that is our etheric body. When we physically die, our "ghost" is freed from our body, along with our spirit. The spirits I communicate with have already crossed over; they aren't in limbo. They absolutely know they're dead. Reviewing their life on Earth, they've realized that they have unresolved issues with the living they'd like to resolve sooner than later, and come through instead of waiting for the living to die so they can make amends. Earthbound ghosts, however, are another story. In the event of a violent, sudden, or tragic death, a spirit may be unaware that he or she is dead, confused, angry, or afraid, and resist going toward the light. These earthbound ghosts are stuck between this Earth plane and the spiritual plane. It is only once they're ready to "wake up" that they'll be able to cross over and be free. Often they need help with this and that's when psychic mediums like the "Ghost Whisperer" help them transition.

AFFIRMATION

I only allow in pure positive energy, light, love, and spirits that are the highest good to me.

What This Means for You: There's no reason to be afraid of lower energies, like earthbound ghosts, for one main reason: *We are always in control of who and what we allow into our life experience.* In other words, you won't attract a yucky poltergeist unless you open yourself up to it. *When we set our intention to allow only loving and light energy into our space, we close the door to ghosts and earthbound spirits.* That said, if we don't invite

There's Nothing to Be Afraid Of

f you are someone who is loving, positive, and kind, you have nothing to worry about. Light attracts light, so if that's what you're projecting out into the world, dark energy won't want anything to do with you. But maybe you're wondering, *What about the nice girl in the horror film terrorized by evil spirits?* That's just Hollywood exploiting our fear. If you stay centered in love and light, you can't be brought down by lower, darker energy. That's not to say you won't encounter it, because you might. In that instance, do as I did in yoga class—send your light, and you'll either transform their darkness or drive them away. In either case, you're safe!

them in and they *still* come through, we reserve the right to ignore them or tell them to go away. Most souls will respect this request. It takes a tremendous amount of energy to come through and appear, so if we refuse to listen to or acknowledge them, most spirits won't waste any more energy on us. It's a lost cause!

Hold On! I Still Don't Get It: Back to the good guys. If I get a spiritual "sign," how do I know if it came from a passed loved one, my spirit guide, or an angel?

Here's the Deal: As long as you intuitively feel that the energy and insight are loving and good, it's not imperative you know what type of spiritual being is providing it. But if you really want to know, just ask! As you get more acquainted with working with various spirits, you'll start to feel the difference in their energies. It's really no different than the living people you interact with. Everyone has a unique energy or "vibe" they give off.

Dead people often use a "sign" to tell you that they're around. Angels and guides often use symbols or names to indicate their presence, and once you figure out what that symbol is, they'll start using it all the time.

For example, your deceased mother may use the smell of her favorite perfume as a sign because she knows you always associate it with her. My grandma Babe often used a Baby Ruth candy bar or the baseball player as a sign when she really needed to get my attention. (Grandma Babe's real name was *Ruth*!) I would find the candy bar wrapper in weird public places or randomly come across some mention of Babe Ruth, and over time, I came to understand that this was her way of saying, *Hello, Rebecca—I need you to check in with me!*

What This Means for You: If you want to establish a relationship with your spiritual guides and angels—you know, introduce yourself and get to know them—try connecting through meditation, dreams, walking in nature, or just having a conversation with them. Find what feels right for you. Some clients even write letters to their spirit guides and then wait for a response. If none of that works, try the following grounding meditation.

MEDITATION

Meet Your Guides

What you'll need: Fifteen minutes and a place to sit or lie comfortably.

Start with your simple breathing meditation. Once you feel grounded and connected to the Earth and your higher self is awakened, imagine yourself in a beautiful setting where you want to meet your spirit guide. Envision a specific spot where you'll meet up each time you want to connect. (For me, this is a deck overlooking the ocean with the sun going down. I put my-self in this scene and drink in the sights, sounds, and smells of this moment. When I'm in this place, I feel free from the past and from expectations of the future.)

Breathe and meditate on this spot for a few minutes.

Ask mentally or aloud, "Who are you? How do you work with me? What do you want to teach me? Do you have any messages for me?" Mentally ask your guide to respond and to identify himself or herself with a name or a symbol.

Then LISTEN!

Pay attention to all your senses—not just your dominant Clair. You may get a visual response such as a flash of light. You may hear a whisper or get a strong feeling or knowing. Don't worry if this doesn't happen right away. It will get easier to connect.

When I'm in this meditation, I sit for a minute or two in the com-fortable deck chair in my mind, feeling relaxed and totally present in the moment. Then a combination of deceased relatives, angels, and guides meet me on the deck. These light beings gather around me in a circle and encourage me to unload. I release my fears, concerns, and anxieties. Once I've emptied out all my frazzled en-ergy, I let their white light of love and truth fill me up. I imagine light coming in through the palms of my outstretched hands and Mind's Eye, inflating me like a white wave. As the light pours in, I receive thoughts, feelings, symbols, and words of guidance. Sometimes it's like watching a movie play out at high speed in my mind. Whatever form it takes, I make a conscious effort to stay open and let it all pour in without criticism or editing.

When the process is complete (this could be five minutes or an hour later), they slowly pull back their light and disappear and leave me alone in my special place. I come back to the awareness of my body and my breath and feel WIDE AWAKE. I'm recharged and reconnected, and even though my spiritual guides are gone for the moment, I don't feel alone. I feel loved, supported, and alive.

Put Spirit to the Test

I know, I know, sometimes a feeling isn't enough—you want proof! If over time, the guide meditation above hasn't convinced you that you're connecting with your guide, then put Spirit to the test. Go into meditation and ask for specific information about yourself or a particular situation you're dealing with. Write down whatever comes to mind (remember, no self-editing: Don't let your mind get involved and start analyzing or exaggerating) and I bet that in the days/weeks to come you'll see evidence to validate your answers one way or another. If that's not enough, you can ask for a particular sign—something that will let you know when they're present with you. But here's the catch: You have to let Spirit determine what the sign will be versus *you* dictating to Spirit what you want it to be. How do you do that? You guessed it! Meditation, what else? Ask your guides to show you what their sign is for you. This sign will appear to you as a mental vision, be heard as a word in your mind's voice, come as an out-of-the-blue knowing, or be felt as a strong feeling. Take whatever is revealed and imagine it coming to you, give thanks for it showing itself, then let go. Next, stay aware in the coming days and weeks for the sign to present itself to you. Now that doesn't mean you go looking for it. If Spirit shows you a clover, for example, don't head down to the nearest Irish bar and announce, "There it is—my cloverleaf sign!"

Early on in my practice, I asked my spirit guide to validate that what I was seeing and receiving in meditation was real and not in my imagination. I got the strong sense of a sunflower. Two days later, a client walked into my office holding a single sunflower out to me. Startled, I said, "Thank you, but why are you giving this to me?" She said, "I really don't know. I just passed by a flower stand on the way here and felt like I should bring you a sunflower." *I'm not kidding—this really happened!* So, give it a try.

Hold On! I Don't Get It: How will I know that the things I'm seeing, hearing, feeling, or just knowing are intuitive messages from Spirit? In other words, how do I know that I'm not just making circumstances fit?

Here's the Deal: Remember that the early stages of this process will require patience as you develop your intuitive sense. You'll have to overcome two common challenges as you get your feet wet:

CHALLENGE #1

Mind Control

The first challenge lies within you—you *must* learn to distinguish between a *mind thought* and an *intuitive thought*. A mind thought is a trailed thought, where you think of something, which leads to another thought, and another and another. You may think you've arrived at an intuitive truth—*Aha!*—except when you trace this thought back to its origin, you'll clearly see that it was manufactured by your analytical mind—the part of your brain that really likes to be in control. Meanwhile, an intuitive thought just pops in from out of the blue, with nothing attached to it.

Making Things Fit

The second challenge lies outside of your mind—the hard task of differentiating between plain old *natural* occurrences and *spirit* activity. For example, your toilet might suddenly gurgle and flush, or your bathtub might start running for no apparent reason. While this may seem odd, this doesn't necessarily mean Spirit is attempting to communicate with you. There may be an explanation for this—like maybe you need a plumber to take a look at your pipes! So, before you call your best friend and declare, *I've made contact with the spirit world*, be sure to rule out all practical explanations, rather than trying to make things fit.

Signs generally appear when we aren't looking for them. They fall into our lap or stare us in the face at just the right time with no reasonable explanation to rule them out as mere coincidence. Signs often appear after a recent or immediate conversation, mental or verbal, about a dead loved one, or after we've prayed to them. For example, not too long ago, I had tea with my friend Sheila. During our time together, I talked about missing my dad, the impact he'd had on my life and my spiritual work. After we said good-bye, I got into my car and turned on the radio, and John Mayer was singing, "Fathers Be Good to Your Daughters," and I thought, *Oh, I can't bear to listen to this. Thanks anyway, Dad!* I immediately turned the dial to another station just as The Fray's "How to Save a Life" came on. This is *the* song that always makes Brian and me think of my dad, so it was as if Dad was saying, "You can't get away from me. Here's my sign and I am with you." It made me smile and cry at the same time.

When you go about your day-to-day business, doing your exercises and opening yourself up to intuitive thought but not forcing it, events and messages will appear organically. That said, don't expect a major shift in your perception overnight. Like any workout, it takes a while to see results. But my guess is that before you know it, you'll be calling your girlfriend and saying, *You're never going to believe this, but the strangest thing just happened to me . . .*

Still unsure about how it works? Take a look at the following signs and how I distinguish between the two:

NO, it's not a sign:

1) Weird noises on several CD recordings of client readings. It was the battery malfunctioning, not Spirit.

2) Lightbulb goes out. It's an old bulb that needs changing.

3) Cell phone drops a call. Sometimes we're in an area with poor reception!

4) Find a penny on the ground while walking outside. Random, not Spirit.

5) You see a bird on your balcony railing. We all see birds. It's not Spirit.

YES, it's a sign:

1) A heartbeat comes through on a CD recording after my client mentions the spirit of her stillborn child. No other heartbeat sound on any other client CDs that day.

2) Brand-new lightbulbs keep bursting or going out every time a client thinks of his deceased wife.

3) Brand-new cell phone keeps malfunctioning. When you take it back to the store, they can't find anything wrong with it.

4) You find a penny on your car seat (and you know you did not drop it there) right after praying or talking to a passed loved one and asking for a sign that everything will be okay.

5) A good friend of yours who passed away loved hummingbirds. You're walking down the street and a hummingbird literally flies into your face!

LEARN THE LANGUAGE

I can almost hear you saying, *Okaaay . . . I* think *I understand how spirit communication works, but how about some more tangible examples?*

You got it. The following is a list of specific ways spirit energy taps us on the shoulder, trying to get our attention. Once you become more aware of how Spirit tries to connect with you, the less likely you'll be to miss messages when they come a tappin'!

As you experience different forms of spirit communication, don't worry about whether your sign or experience "works" for others. Remember—you are on your *own* path to clarity.

Animals

Animals often pick up on spirit energy, mainly because they're highly sensitive and their minds don't interfere like ours by doubting, analyzing, or judging. When your pet looks like it's watching an invisible fly move around the room; when it whimpers or growls in a particular direction;

when it acts as if it's playing with someone, running in circles, jumping all over the place, or swatting the air—it may be recognizing spirit energy. Sure, a lot of times animals just behave this way. But when unusual behavior is accompanied by your intuitive feeling that there's energy in the room with you, it's very possible Spirit is communicating with your pet as a means to get your attention.

Appliances

With enough focused energy, Spirit can manipulate electrical appliances. They simply cross their energy with the electrical energy fueling the machine, causing interference with its normal operation. They may choose to mess with appliances that you use daily in an effort to get your attention. Examples include turning on the coffeemaker, flickering the refrigerator light, or changing the timer on the microwave. This could easily be an energy surge, a short, or a faulty appliance, but when the "weirdness" happens repeatedly and at random, it's most likely spirit energy trying to connect. Use your best judgment. Note that Spirit may also direct their energy into a particular room where they spent a lot of time in life, such as the kitchen, or if they know you spend most of your time in one room, they are likely to show up in that location.

Art

Spirit energy can communicate through one's artistic abilities in an attempt to offer guidance. When this happens, you may feel a very strong and spontaneous need to be creative, with no real conscious thought of what you're creating. *Why did I just pull out my watercolor set?* Spirit will often inspire you to paint, draw, sculpt, or create a piece of art as a means to trigger a moment of understanding about your life.

Automatic Writing

If you enjoy writing, automatic writing can be a powerful and effective way to communicate with Spirit. Start by journaling your heartfelt thoughts and feelings and ask your mind to let go and not interfere. As you write, it may start to feel like an outside energy is pulling your hands across the page or keyboard. Go with it. The messages may be cryptic in the beginning, but with practice and an increased comfort level, the process, along with the messages, should become more fluent and clear. Don't be alarmed if you notice a difference in handwriting style from your own, along with a distinct difference in wording.

Books and Other Printed Matter

Spirit may speak to you through written material, including books, magazines, newspapers, notes, or letters. You'll often stumble upon these random messages with no conscious thought, although finding them typically follows a request for guidance from Spirit. You may feel drawn to pull a certain book off the bookshelf, a certain headline or caption in the newspaper may catch your eye; you may find a flyer or a scrap of paper on the ground while walking down the street and feel compelled to pick it up. Regardless of the way you come across this material, recognize that Spirit is inspiring you to see and read an important message.

Bugs and Birds

No, I don't believe that your deceased loved one is literally coming back as a fly! Rather, I've observed that Spirit sometimes manipulates the energy of these winged ones to cross our paths and get our attention. Again, there's a fine line between the ordinary and the extraordinary. There are a lot of bugs and birds out there! It's up to you to decide if the experience is spiritual in nature—Do cardinals hold special significance for you? Did one fly past your window five times today? Look for symbolism and repetition. For example, during a reading I once did for a young woman, her father came through and mentioned her recent wedding. He had died shortly after she got engaged. When he asked her if she liked the butterfly he sent, she burst into tears. She told me that during her wedding ceremony, while she and her soon-to-be-husband stood at the altar, a butterfly flew around them for several minutes capturing the attention of everyone in the congregation. At the time, she felt like it was the presence of her father offering his blessing; he knew how much she loved butterflies because he'd always loved them, too.

Celebrations

When family and friends get together for significant and happy occasions, spirit energy is often present. Why? Because at these times, positive energy tends to fill and surround each person, drawing Spirit in. This is especially true when people gather and reminisce over happy times shared with passed loved ones—it's like an open invitation for Spirit to join the party. During family get-togethers, I like to make a toast to all my loved ones—past and present.

◆ TESTIMONIAL

I had a reading with Rebecca in July 2001. When my husband, Steve, came through in spirit, he promised that he would make his presence known in the form of a white dove.

The following April, a white dove appeared on my front porch. It stayed there for about two weeks, through what would have been our wedding anniversary, April 24! I saw it as his way of acknowledging the special date and to deliver the message that his love for me is still present and strong, as is mine for him!
—*Anne from Detroit, Michigan*

Children

Have you ever noticed that kids can say the most amusing—and oddly insightful—things? Young children often act as unconscious messengers for Spirit. Their minds and hearts are open, which keeps them free of judgment and doubt. Spirit has an easier time connecting with children because they're more fully in the present moment, free from regrets of the past or worry and anticipation about the future. Children tend to speak without questioning where the thought or insight is coming from; their imaginations are often full of wisdom and truth.

For example, one afternoon when I was very close to my delivery date for my second baby, my son Jakob said to me, "Grandpa Shelly came to me when I was drinking my milk this morning and said he'd be in the room when Mommy has the baby." I was dumbfounded. Just that morning, Dad had visited me in a meditation and told me the exact same thing. I hadn't shared this message with anyone and then Jakob validated it unknowingly!

Chills (Angel Bumps)

When Spirit is around us, we may *feel* the higher vibration and get "the chills." If we acknowledge our feelings and thoughts in that moment, we may be able to tune in to whomever the energy belongs to, be it an angel, spirit guide, or deceased loved one. If we're unsure, we can ask—*Who are you and what message do you have for me?* Pay attention to the thought, feeling, or emotion that immediately follows your request. *Did you get your answer?*

Clairgustance—Clear Tasting

This sense occurs when we taste a food, drink, or other substance inspired by Spirit to communicate symbolic information. True story: I was in the middle of a reading when the spirit of a woman came through, and all the references she offered made no sense to my client. Add to that, this spirit would not offer me her name. After several minutes of pondering, I mentally asked the spirit to show me one thing or memory that would make it clear to my client who she was. She then inspired a taste in my mouth of pad thai. I asked my client what it meant and the reference immediately drew her to her deceased friend. They used to have lunch every Monday at their favorite Thai restaurant, where her friend always ordered pad thai!

Coins

Spirit can inspire coins to appear in random and unusual places as a way to get our attention—often as a message of prosperity. Because coins, especially pennies, are often found lying around in the home, at the bottom of your purse, or in the subway station, it may be hard to distinguish between spirit energy and chance circumstance. So, pay attention to patterns and specific coins that consistently reappear. For example, my dad and his second wife had a significant connection to the number eleven. They would often find eleven cents, a dime and a penny together in totally random places, and felt convinced that Spirit was using this coin combo to make its presence known. After my dad passed away, I started coming across the same dime and penny combination. Because it was never significant to me before, I came to believe that Dad was using one of his favorite signs to remind me of him.

Cooking

Cooking is a love and a passion for many people because it can be so therapeutic and creative. If the kitchen is a positive space for you—a place where you allow yourself to relax and quiet your mind—it's highly likely that Spirit will visit you there. The next time you're preparing a dish, focus on staying present and open to your intuition. You may experience a strong feeling of energy surrounding you or notice odd things happening in the kitchen, like an electrical interference or a sudden inspiration to cook a particular dish—a favorite recipe of a loved one who has passed. *Beef Stroganoff, anyone?*

One of my clients once had her extended family over for Sunday brunch just months after her father died. She felt her father's presence in the kitchen as she prepared the bagels and lox. A few days later when she came in for her reading, her father came through and mentioned the "bagels and lox," validating that he had been with her that Sunday morning in the kitchen.

Dreams

When you sleep, your outer mind can rest, and your inner subconscious mind is finally able to speak. Spirit is more likely to communicate with you in this altered state because your mind is open. When we're visited by Spirit in our dreams, the imagery tends to be very vivid, leaving you with a feeling of deep knowing and reconnection. Haven't you ever woken up from a dream and said, "Well, that was interesting! I wonder what *that* means?" If it's not totally clear, write the dream down. You'll sometimes find aspects of the dream will play out in the physical world.

Not All Dreams Are Created Equal

Since our dreams can be so varied, here are some distinctions you can begin to make:

1) **Visitations:** A visitation dream is when we get an actual visit from a spirit to reassure us that he or she has successfully passed on. Visitations tend to feel very real, and the memory of the dream often stays with us for a long time after waking, if not indefinitely.

2) **Prophetic Dreams:** A prophetic dream is when we tap into Source energy and receive information about the future (like my dream about Grandpa Harold and moving to California).

3) **Angelic/Guide Connection:** Angels and spirit guides use the dream state to send messages to us or help us heal our damaged energy. You may awaken and feel like something has shifted in the night. You feel lighter, clearer, and happier for no apparent reason.

Make More of Your Dreams

One way to increase your chances of having a prophetic dream or visitation is by setting your intention. You want to plant the seed in your consciousness, especially if you don't normally remember your dreams. Before going to sleep, mentally or verbally invite Spirit into your dreams. I say this prayer:

> Angels, guides, and loved ones: Thank you for meeting me in my dreams tonight. I welcome your guidance, wisdom, healing

energy, and love. I intend to wake up feeling clear, balanced, and spiritually aligned.

Be patient. This muscle takes time to develop like any other. It may not happen overnight, but with your active willingness and intention, you'll most likely start having powerful, vivid dreams that you'll recall after waking.

Ears Ringing

When your ears start ringing, even though you don't hear a loud noise, you can be pretty certain that Spirit is present. Ringing in your ears results from a change in air pressure and can indicate a spirit's energy shifting and tapping into your own. Make note of what you're thinking or feeling when your ears begin to ring—it's likely that Spirit is simply checking in.

Electricity

It's easy for Spirit to manipulate electricity because both of these forms of energy vibrate at a higher frequency—they "speak" the same language. Look for lights flickering in the house, lightbulbs blowing out, disturbance with television sets, radios, and computers. Yes, every electrical appliance has the potential of going bonkers from time to time, but when malfunctions happen repeatedly and without any other explanation, it's safe to bet that Spirit is trying to get your attention.

True Stories: Electricity

I was once reading a woman when her husband came through. He said he'd attempted contact by messing with the lights and other electrical appliances in the house and told his wife that she needed to get her bedroom light fixture replaced. She was stunned when she heard this because the lights *had* been operating erratically since the day he died. She reported waking up in the middle of the night to find the bedroom light turned on and that the ceiling fan had begun turning off and on by itself. Once I relayed her husband's message, all of this electrical mischief made perfect sense to her—of course her husband would choose to contact her with electricity; he'd spent his career as an electrician.

Film, TV, and Theater

Spirit may inspire you to watch a particular movie, TV show, or theater performance in an attempt to convey a significant message that you need to hear. I did a reading for a woman who mentioned that *The Wizard of Oz* had been a favorite of hers and her mother's. Ever since her mother's death, she told me, she'd watch it when she wanted to feel the presence of her mom. Well, the evening after our reading, my client went home and turned on the TV just as the opening credits for *The Wizard of Oz* began. She knew this was her mom saying hello and validating that the movie was an ongoing sign of her presence.

Flowers and Gardens

Nature, especially flowers and trees, has a high vibrational frequency similar to spirit energy. If Spirit knows you enjoy being at the park, walking around on your lunch break, or gardening, it's likely that Spirit will attempt to connect with you when you're enjoying the outdoors. Become mindful of your thoughts and feelings when you're digging in the dirt or clipping flowers.

Furniture

Spirit can cause subtle physical impressions on furniture, making it feel like someone has just sat down next to you, moved around, or gotten up. Most likely, the spirit energy of a loved one is simply visiting—he or she misses you! If this sounds unbelievable, listen to this story about my good friend Katie, who's a bit of a skeptic by nature. A couple of years after her dad died, Katie felt lonely and was often depressed. One night, she remembers going to bed thinking about her dad and mentally telling him how much she loved and missed him. She fell asleep on her side and hours later, she woke up feeling as if someone was standing in the room. She was too spooked to turn over and see if anyone was there, so she stayed still. Then she felt someone lie down beside her. At that moment she just *knew* that it was her dad. Mind you, she was wide awake, but felt like she was dreaming. Minutes later, the feeling left, but not the sense that her father had just been there.

Gifts

Spirit sometimes brings gifts into our lives to serve as a reminder that we are loved. The gift usually shows up as a random act of kindness we didn't expect or even asked for! For example, I once did a reading for a man whose brother had died years before. In the reading, I told him that his brother had sent him a gift—something about jalapeño peppers. He completely flipped out when he made the connection. He had just received a gift basket of assorted jalapeño peppers with no card attached. He had no idea where it came from until his brother tipped him off in the reading.

Knock on Wood

Talk about tapping! This form of communication happens when spirit energy makes noises like a knock on wood, furniture, and walls, or like electrical snaps in the air. It's like—*Hello, is anybody out there?* Again, rule out all practical explanations for this type of occurrence before attributing it to spirit energy. Ask yourself, *Is it happening often, at the same time of day or night? Is it happening just after a thought or conversation about a dead loved one? Is the noise unique in sound, pattern, or rhythm?* If you answered YES to the above, it's most likely a sign from Spirit.

License Plates and Numbers

Do you have a favorite number or number sequence? Spirit will often use number patterns that hold meaning for you to attempt contact. What to look for: random lotto numbers, license plate numbers, times on a clock, receipt totals, birth dates, or other significant dates.

Because Spirit is often with us while we're driving, synchronistic events with license plates are common occurrences if we pay attention to them. What to look for: frequent and consistent number patterns, vanity tags, bumper stickers, or any other significant date or meaningful number combinations. But be careful! No need to start looking for these. Just keep your eyes on the road and let them show up.

For example, I was driving home from work one day, listening to a voice mail from a good friend. She said she had something important to share and asked me to call her ASAP. Right then, I pulled up to a stop light behind a license plate that read "BABYGRL." I called her back and sure enough—she told me she was pregnant with a baby girl.

Mail

Spirit may inspire mail to come into our lives as a way to offer support at just the right time. It usually happens in response to a request for guidance regarding the next step in our lives. It could be an e-mail announcing a new book coming out—one which we would greatly benefit from reading—an inspiring newsletter that pops up at the perfect time, addressing a specific issue we are struggling with, a card sent by a friend when we're in need of support or advice, or an unexpected check or refund at a time when we really need the money.

Music

Music, like spirit energy, has a high vibration. This match in frequency makes it easy for Spirit to tap in to radio waves. What to look for: a radio turning on by itself, a song that reminds us of a passed loved one at the exact time we are thinking about him or her, or a song popping into our head that offers the message we need to hear.

Night Waking

When our minds are sleepy, it's much easier for Spirit to get through to us. Have you ever woken up in the middle of the night for no apparent reason? When this happens, if you can pull yourself out of bed to

What Happens When the Spirits Disappoint?

Even I have to constantly remind myself that the spirits don't always tell us what we want to hear or what we think we should hear, but only what we really need to know. Why? Because we can't see the big picture and more often than not, if information is revealed to us that appears distasteful, uncomfortable, or tragic, we're likely to try to change the outcome, in effect altering how events are supposed to play out and interfering in the intended order of things.

Case in point: A couple finds out that they're pregnant, and a few months into the pregnancy, doctors tell them that the baby will likely be born with Down Syndrome. They are devastated by the news. They have no other children and very much want to begin a family, but they're scared of the predicted outcome. They consider all possibilities, including aborting the baby, but they wonder, *What if the baby is born perfectly fine?*

While they're trying to make this difficult decision, Albert (a client of mine and a cousin to this couple) has a prophetic dream about the pregnancy. The following passage is what he recorded in his dream journal.

I do not know how long after I fell asleep that I began to dream. I notice a big warehouse with a single light source hitting the center of the space . . . I walk toward it and notice it's more like a TV studio set and a woman is standing in the middle of it. Her back is toward me and she is singing a familiar song: "*Que sera, sera*—whatever will be, will be." As I approach her, I notice that this woman is none other than Doris Day! I greet her and she says, "So, I see, you want to know something. Don't you know that the future is not for all to see and here you are asking questions." I don't know what to say, but I am eager to talk to her some more. She continues, "Everything will be fine. The real reason for the birth of a child is to bring love and affection. This experience will allow [your cousin] to learn what it means to love someone in a devoted manner. It will bring everyone closer together based on that love." She asks, "Do you want to see the baby?"

She turns around in a circle and by the time she is facing me again she is holding a baby in her arms. The baby looks at peace. She smiles and says, "See, he is a fine boy. Nothing wrong. You should know he comes with a Merrill Lynch warranty."

A little bewildered, I ask, "Merrill Lynch? What the heck does Merrill Lynch have to do with the baby?"

She smiles at the baby and I can clearly see the resemblance of my cousin Fernando. She tells me once more, "The baby comes with warranty. He will be fine." Then she turns and walks away singing, "Que sera, sera."

A moment later I wake up feeling happy knowing that I am able to be a messenger and deliver a little peace of mind to my cousin. Now all I have to do is call him and ask him if he knows if the baby is a boy. Only then will I feel that this information is the special message he was waiting for.

What Albert soon learned was that indeed, his cousin was expecting a boy and that the night before his prophetic dream, his cousin and his wife had argued, once again, over the decision to see the pregnancy through or abort the baby. Frustrated, Fernando had shouted, "I cannot offer you a warranty like those of Merrill Lynch!"

After hearing about his cousin's dream, Fernando and his wife felt relief that their baby would be healthy and fine and decided to continue the pregnancy. Several months later, their son was born with a disability, but Fernando and his wife express no regrets. Instead, they were immediately grateful for their son and insist that he has brought a level of love and closeness to the household that they did not have before. They could not be happier.

meditate or write, you're making the highest use of the experience, allowing for guidance and clarity. Usually, this pattern of waking will stop once you've been able to work through your struggle.

Objects on the Move

An "apport" object is one that Spirit has moved or manipulated. Often, it's a meaningful or valuable object placed in your path, a personal possession out of place, or a specific item in your home, car, or desk that reminds you of a passed loved one. Spirits may communicate with us by repeatedly bringing objects to our attention that held significance to them when they were alive.

For example, one week after my father died, I returned to my medium work. I was experiencing a roller coaster of emotions, doubtful of my intuitive abilities at a time that was so sad and heartbreaking for me. When I got to my office, I waited for the elevator, but it was taking much longer than usual, so I decided to take the stairs instead. When I opened the door to the stairwell, I noticed a nail on the first step with a piece of carpet wrapped around it—it looked like a bow. I cried and thanked my dad for such a clear message. In life, my dad's favorite symbol was a nail. He even wrote a book titled *A Nail in the Road*. I believe it was his way of applauding me for picking myself up after such a tragedy and showing up to serve others.

Phone Calls

This is rare, but sometimes Spirit will use a direct phone line to relay messages to a loved one. The call can range from static to one fuzzy word to an hour of clear conversation. As incredible as this sounds, it's possible to do when a spirit focuses enough energy and intention. For example, I was reading a woman who lost her son in an accident just one year before our session. During the reading, her son mentioned that he had messed with her cell phone to let her know that he was okay. She was stunned. She went on to tell me that shortly after he died, she found *one missed call* appearing on her phone log. When she checked who it was from, her son's name appeared even though his phone service had been disconnected immediately after his death.

Photography

Sometimes after developing film or viewing a digital image, we can see spirit energy in the photo that was invisible to the eye when the picture was taken. What to look for: streaks of light, circular balls of light known as orbs, facial features, or even outlines of bodies. For example, I had a client who shared a photograph with me that she had taken in her living room. She captured an incredibly vivid picture of her deceased father on the screen of the television set, which was turned off. It showed him sitting down in his chair, as he always did, with one hand on his cane. She said it was exactly how he used to sit in his chair. She was in amazement, but also comforted by the visit.

Scent

Have you ever noticed a strong smell, an odor or fragrance wafting around you, with no indication of where it was coming from? This could be spirit energy connecting you to a passed loved one who had a strong and consistent scent associated with him or her; it could be a perfume, cologne, cigarette odor, or any other distinguishable and unique scent.

A client once shared with me that after her father's death, she was desperate for a sign from him. Her father had died of lung cancer from years of smoking, so naturally the smell of cigarettes disgusted her, but she couldn't deny that every time she smelled smoke, she was reminded of her father. One day when she was driving with her young daughter, she got a sudden and strong whiff of cigarette smoke. This made no sense to her. *Where was the smell coming from?* But she was sure of it—she smelled tobacco all around her. Minutes later her daughter said, "Poppy says he loves you!" My client burst into tears of gratitude. *Poppy* was what her daughter called her father.

Signage

Sometimes Spirit shows up as literal *signs* that stand out to capture our attention. These signs, billboards, ads, flyers, generally address a specific question we want an answer to. Signage is everywhere so it's up to us to discern the difference between messages that are inspired or uninspired.

On the night of my thirty-first birthday, my husband and I went out to dinner. As we were leaving the restaurant, I mentally asked Dad to send me a sign that he was with us. As we walked along, Brian and I began debating whether to go to a movie. I thought about it for a minute and then told Brian that I was *feeling* we were supposed to go, although I had no idea why. So, we made our way toward the theater located directly across from a small strip mall—the only visible sign said "NAIL" in huge letters. It became very clear that Dad wanted us to go to the theater simply to see the nail sign and know he was with us!

Sounds

Spirit can interfere with objects that make sound, causing us to stop and take note. This usually happens when we're absolutely quiet, so that a random noise will get our full attention. What to listen for: clock radios, alarms, audible toys, the volume on televisions and radios, computer speakers, car radios, and doorbells.

Temperature Change

The presence of Spirit is often associated with temperature change because in order for Spirit to manifest in the physical world, a tremendous amount of energy is required. So, watch when it becomes very cold in certain spots within a room.

Watches

A recurring pattern on a particular clock or watch is often used by Spirit to get our attention. What to look for: A watch may suddenly stop at a specific time or start working again after a long period of being broken. We may repeatedly see the same time, day and night, when we think to check the time. We may wake up night after night at the exact same time.

True Stories: Watches

I had a client whose father came through during her reading and referenced his broken watch. My client explained that her dad hadn't worn a watch for many years before his death, but that she and her mother had found an old watch of his not long after his funeral. It had stopped at exactly 11:11, the exact time her father was pronounced dead. Ever since, she said the number pattern had shown up in other ways, such as on receipts. When this happens, my client explained, she feels it's the presence of her father.

Hold On! I Don't Get It: I love the idea of becoming aware of the presence of Spirit—like my great-grandmother visiting me in the kitchen—but I'm not sure how this translates to advice.

Here's the Deal: Spirit is always trying to get our attention, but most of us have spent the majority of our lives completely "tuned out" to spirits, unaware of their presence. Once we become tuned in to their incessant tapping, we can begin to ask them to get involved in our lives.

What This Means for You: With a strong sense of trust and belief, you'll start to notice Spirit where you hadn't before. And once this happens, feel free to ask away. Ask Spirit to guide you, to bring you clarity, to help you move forward. Put your heart into your request, stay present, and be open to what messages you receive.

Once you become aware of how the spirit world talks to you, recognizing the signs all around you, it's hard not to feel a little more connected to everything and everyone. Signs from Spirit build your faith that your life has purpose, and knowing this, you can move forward with less hesitation and fear. And while it's absolutely true that spirit energy is available to help and guide you past your current challenges and struggles, this doesn't mean that you won't have to do a lot of work on your own. But you're a strong person—someone who won't give up until you have the life you want—so roll up your sleeves and let's get to work!

6

✳

Do the Work

Intuitive clarity and spiritual awareness put us back in the driver's seat and on the road to a happy, healthy life, but not without doing the maintenance work. *You* have to do your own work in order to heal. The goal of this chapter is to outline

- Mental,
- Emotional,
- Physical, and
- Spiritual strategies for moving forward and fulfilling your life's purpose.

Doing the work will look different to each one of you, but the goal for all of us is the same: shake off the past, drop worries about the future, and get present. When we're present, we grow our intuitive power and evolve on a soul level.

Doing my own work began with a deliberate shift in the way I thought. Because I'd sunk so low into my depression and self-destructive behavior, I knew I had to discipline myself if I wanted to see real change. With regular meditation and journaling, I was able to reprogram my inner dialogue, shift my mind away from negative thoughts, and focus on attracting better experiences into my life. In addition to thinking differently, I worked hard at cleaning up my physical routine; I eliminated all junk food and caffeine from my diet (those afternoon double cappuccinos had to go!). The intensity of my work went on for about a year and a half. *Yes—it took that long.* And I continue to actively do my own work every day. Undoing a lifetime of unhealthy patterns doesn't happen overnight. It's like keeping your house clean and organized—there's *always* work to be done and an ongoing to-do list to tackle. But isn't it a great feeling to check things off the list instead of letting the gunk pile up? *The reward is the ongoing practice.*

But maybe you're wondering, *How does the average working woman, busy mom, and wife make time for daily, personal work?* It's not easy. I have to juggle a schedule just like you and there are days, believe me, when the idea of taking thirty minutes for myself seems like an impossibility. But I make it work, and it's worth it. It'll be important for you to determine your own "spiritual schedule"—how you incorporate your spiritual life into your daily routine.

DAY TO DAY

I don't just intend to stay present throughout the day, I *plan* for it. Before I get out of bed in the morning, I quietly linger under the covers for about thirty seconds to a minute. I pray for intuitive clarity and guidance as I make decisions throughout the day. I mentally invite my guides, angels, and spirits to come in and be present with me. My prayer often sounds something like this, *Please help me get out of my own way today. Please take away my fear and anxiety and fill me with peace. Inspire me to be the best version of myself. Use me how you need me to help other people.* By doing this, I'm setting a positive intention for the day. You'll have your own version.

Next, I do a little psychic shielding. I envision a shell of protective white light surrounding me throughout the day. I mentally say, *Thank you for watching over me today. Please extend my love and protective light to everyone in my life.*

Then I get up and positively line up my day. Nearly every morning I go to the gym and hop on the elliptical machine or the treadmill. (For me, the gym is a win-win. I can be physical and spiritual at the same time.) For the first five to ten minutes of my warm-up, I mentally go through my to-do list for the day. I imagine leaving the gym after my workout, meeting with clients, picking my son up from school, running errands, making dinner, and so on. As I run through the list, I imagine everything working out positively and according to plan (I'm on time, I make meaningful connections for my clients, my son is in a great mood, etc.). Then after I've spent several minutes setting this positive intention, I release control of the eventual outcome. I mentally ask (God, Source, the Universe) to let my day unfold just as it should—not necessarily how I *think* it will—and then I commit to staying present for the rest of the day.

Often when I'm doing my elliptical meditation, I look around at my fellow gym rats who I imagine are doing the same thing—mentally planning for their day. But I can guarantee you that almost all of them are worrying about what will go *wrong*, instead of what will go *right*. Most of us don't know to trust that our lives will unfold in perfect order without our constant attention and involvement. (It's a good thing you know better than that now!) When we can't let go of our need to control, it's nearly impossible to be in the *now* moment, and inevitably, we set ourselves up for disappointment.

Once I'm done at the gym, I go home, get ready for work, drop my older son off at school and my younger one with the sitter, and head to the office. I usually have about twenty minutes before I have my first reading, so I spend that time meditating and clearing my energy. Once again, I invite in Spirit to protect and work with me and use me as an instrument of peace, clarity, and healing.

At the end of my workday, I take fifteen minutes to release all the energy that I've absorbed from Spirit and my clients. I ask for my energy back and visualize letting theirs go. I mentally put the CLOSED sign up—you know, the one that says, "Thanks. Come again!" Sometimes, if I have time, I go to a yoga class to further release my energy and clear it for the next day. Finally, I go home and make dinner like many of you, visit with my husband, and play with my sons. The following day, I do it all over again.

This may seem like a lot of time dedicated to spiritual practice, but for me it's the basic maintenance work. But remember, I talk to the dead for a living, so it's part of the job. How much time you commit to intuitively connecting is totally up to you. You may want to adopt elements of my routine or create one totally unique to you. The important thing is to connect on a regular basis until it becomes habit. For some people, this might be once or twice a week. For others it will be once or twice a day.

You see, without regularly checking in, it's easy to get sidetracked and knocked off balance. This goes for me, too. Whenever I have more than a day or two off from work, I become very distracted with earthly concerns and become almost oblivious to Spirit. I get caught up in the material world, worrying about money, my to-do list, relationships, and petty gossip. I'll catch myself going around and around in that spinning wheel of doubt and worry. When I realize my ego has taken over, I have to force myself to snap out of it—*Rebecca, stop going there*—and release my mind control and connect back with my higher self and Spirit. Is it as easy as turning off a switch? If only!

MENTAL WORK

When I talk about mental work, I'm referring to the practice of *mind control* (and no, not the stuff of sci-fi movies). Quite simply, our thoughts can work for us and make us stronger, or they can work against us and make us weaker. You've certainly heard the expression, *Is your cup half-empty or half-*

full? As the saying goes, the people who regard their cup as half-empty looks at life in terms of what's missing. Half-empty folks are ruled by their egos, or their lower selves, and have little trust or belief in the abundance of life. They tend to act from a place of victimization and fear. Half-full people, on the other hand, see what life has to offer and tend to look at life from a position of optimism. Both half-empty and half-full make the choice to think the way they do. Who will attract more positive experiences into their life? Who will be more likely to connect intuitively? Need I ask?

So, what's the takeaway here? Be mindful of your thoughts. If you're a half-empty kind of person, make a conscious effort to change your thinking because those negative mind thoughts are *not* working for you! One of my favorite quotes about mental work is from Albert Einstein. He said, "There are only two ways to live your life: One is though nothing is a miracle. The other is though everything is."

Which life do you want: a life of fear or a life of love? I hope you know you want the latter. You wouldn't be reading this book if you didn't! To live a life of love, you begin by choosing to surround yourself with people and environments that create positive thoughts and feelings in you. For example, I don't watch a lot of television news because, as far as I'm concerned, it's just a laundry list of what's going wrong in the world. It doesn't make me feel good. I get too emotionally attached to the disturbing images, and before I know it, I'm totally freaked out and operating moment to moment out of fear. So, I don't turn it on.

I'm not suggesting that you ignore reality (I still read newspapers and find other ways to check in on the world around me), but that you *limit* your intake of negative energy. I can't deny (nor should I) what's going on in my neighborhood, city, or country, but I can choose how I think about what's going on and how much I think about it. When we choose to focus on poverty, sickness, and unhappiness, we run the risk of attracting these things into our lives. Let me be clear: This is different than having an *awareness* of poverty, sickness, and unhappiness. Here's an example: Our neighborhood recently had a rash of burglaries. For several nights, I worried that our house might be the next one hit. I kept replaying a scene in my head where I wake up and someone is in the house. After about the third night of this, I thought, *Enough! This is someone else's experience. It doesn't have to be mine. I'm going to stop thinking about this and attracting it into my life!* I got out of bed, took a look around the house, and made sure the alarm was on. I got back into bed resolved that I had done all I could do to prevent a break-in. I let it go and stopped thinking about it.

The moment you see your thoughts getting out of control, you have to learn to stop and tell yourself, *I'm not going to play this movie anymore.* The thoughts and visions we repeat in our minds every day are like a mantra. Over time, they will manifest into our physical reality. If you think, *I'm going to get robbed, I'm going to get robbed, I'm going to get robbed . . .* eventually, you're going to get robbed! The Law of Attraction guarantees that we will attract to us what we store in our minds.

Tools for Your Mental Toolbox

In order for us to find that inner place of quiet wisdom and intuitive knowing, we have to clear our minds of negative thoughts and make room for positive ones.

When we cancel negative thoughts, we withdraw our energy from them, much like denying plants water. They eventually wither and die. The repetitive use of positive thinking and affirmations waters new thought seeds in the soil of your subconscious mind. With repeated use, positive affirmations will eventually become automatic behavior, and you will see powerful results bloom in your waking life. That said, even Chia Pets don't mature overnight. Give positive change a chance to grow. Your job is to plant the seeds, shower them with your attention, and then walk away and let nature take its course. Try incorporating any or all of these tools into your routine:

1) **Affirmations:** Create strong positive statements in the present tense, acting as if the experience has already happened. Stand in front of a mirror, look yourself in the eyes, and say your affirmations aloud with conviction. Repeat this process for three weeks until you lose your self-consciousness and there is no resistance. Repeat the statement, mentally and aloud, until it's fully programmed into your subconscious mind.

2) **Creative Visualization:** Thoughts are images we have made in our minds. So, if we can imagine the healed or finished result of an affirmation already taking place, it acts as a direct suggestion to our subconscious mind. Take this scenario for example: You have an upcoming lecture to give that you want to go smoothly. Imagine yourself (create a mental picture in your mind) presenting with grace and ease and conjure up the physical feeling of success—you feel GREAT! I do this all the time. In fact, I do it every day! Before client readings, I imagine a successful day where spirits are lined up and ready to go, I make strong connections with Spirit, and, in turn, my clients are open and receptive to the messages I have for them.

3) **Journaling:** When we write down our affirmations, we are programming the subconscious from yet another direction.

4) **Affirmation Cards:** Write affirmations on cards and place them around your house, work, or vehicle. They serve as reminders to say them and accelerate the process.

5) **Reading:** Reading spiritual and self-help books serves as a powerful programming and patterning device.

6) **Pictures and Vision Boards:** Create a physical picture or a collage of pictures and words that serve as a suggestion of the imagined, desired, or healed result. The images should

provoke a strong positive feeling that in time the subconscious mind will seek to manifest.

7) **Meditation:** Meditation is designed to free your mind from fear-based blocks, allowing your intuitive wisdom to shine through. To specifically clear your mind of negative mojo and make room for positive thought, try the Let Go and Fill Up and Planting the Seeds meditations on pages 232 and 237 at the back of the book.

Expand Your Limited Thinking

Creating the lives we want is only limited by our thinking, so think BIG! You are the co-creator of your life. Take a look around you. Your present circumstances are a result of what you've been focusing your attention on, even if you didn't realize it. So, if you don't like what you see, it's time to start thinking differently. I have the following index card hanging in my office as a daily reminder of the role I play in co-creating my life.

How to Manifest a Happy Life

Step One: Be clear about what I want and need.

Step Two: Ask for what I want and need—be specific in my request!

Step Three: Believe it's on the way.

Step Four: Live in a state of gratitude . . . *Thank you, thank you, thank you.*

Step Five: Be open to receive what arrives and accept that it is in my highest interest and good.

EMOTIONAL WORK

Relying on your intuitive wisdom to answer your day-to-day questions becomes much easier to do once you've broken down your emotional walls. In Chapter Four: Put Your Past in Your Past, you did much of this work already. You dug in, uncovered the root of your struggle, and began the work of getting present. Regardless, emotional wounds take a while to heal, so as you continue to do the work, give yourself permission to *feel* what you feel. Don't be afraid to let rogue emotions bust through the walls. Have the courage to face them, especially when they're uncomfortable.

This is kind of a gross analogy, but think of your emotional channels like the pipes that carry the dirty water out of your bathtub. Every so often, you have to clean out the drain because it gets clogged with hair, soap, and other gunk. I don't know about you, but this isn't one of my favorite things to do. Still, I know it's necessary so that water can drain and flow freely again. It's the same with your emotional channels: They routinely need to be cleansed so your energy can flow without interruption. When we suppress our feelings, we run the risk of blocking our intuitive voice as well as our hearts. Over time, a blocked heart can lead to depression and disease. And forget about trying to connect with Spirit—it's just not going to happen!

Given my line of work, if I'm not watchful, I'll take on the emotional baggage of everyone around me. I'll just pile it on until I can't stand it. It usually takes about three or four days before I collapse under the weight and emotionally shut down. This is my cue that I need a release, and fast! (Before I start snapping at my poor husband over everything.) So, how do I clean my own emotional channels? It might surprise you that I prefer the old-fashioned method—I break down and cry. Sometimes you just need a good cry, am I right? When crying doesn't get it all out, I ask

Brian to let me vent. It's a blessing to have a person in your life who's willing to patiently sit and listen while you talk through your feelings.

But I know that for many people it's not as simple as opening up
and unloading. Sometimes, you won't even know you're emotionally
blocked until something seemingly innocent, like a song or a newspaper
article, suddenly triggers a feeling, and the next thing you know, you've
become an emotional wreck. Not to worry. The following are a few tools
for opening up your heart in a safe and controlled environment so that
you're not suddenly caught off-guard by a surge of emotion while you're
in the checkout line.

Tools for Your Emotional Toolbox

If you're having trouble clearing your emotional channels, try the exercise
below that goes with your strongest intuitive sense. If feelings rise to the
surface (and that's the point), I encourage you to acknowledge them, take
them into the Heart Opener meditation on page 238 at the back of the
book and release them. It's good to clean out any fear, resentment, or
negativity that you may be holding in your heart. Our heart is the gate-
way to sending and receiving love—and to accessing our intuition.

Clairvoyant: If you're highly visual try watching a heartwarming
movie, pull out meaningful home videos, or look at old pictures.

Clairaudient: If you're an auditory person, talk honestly and openly
with a friend or a loved one or try listening to inspiring music and even sing
along (one of my favorite things to do is sing out loud in my car with the
music on high and the windows rolled up). Getting your feelings down on
paper is also an effective way to get clear and release emotional garbage.

Clairsentient: If you feel things strongly, try spending time with
people who make you feel safe and good about yourself. (Avoid psychic
vampires. They drain your energy.) Playtime with family and friends is
important. Anyone who gets you laughing and feeling joyful helps clear

your emotional channels of negative gunk. Also, spend time in places that make you feel alive and positively charged. For many people, being out in nature allows their true feelings to "naturally" rise to the surface.

Claircognizant: If you're "knowing," try spending some quiet time alone to release and recharge. Most women don't do enough of this. Many of us feel guilty taking time for ourselves and instead focus on taking care of everybody else. But when we neglect ourselves, we become emotionally compromised. Whenever I have a free window of time within my work-day, I take a walk, meditate, or listen to music—anything that allows me to be quiet and alone. Practice saying, *This is my time!*

PHYSICAL WORK

The healthier our physical bodies are, the easier it will be to connect intuitively and heighten our awareness of spirit energy. Doing the physical work means clearing our bodies of spiritual debris and toxic energy that clog, distract, and depress our intuitive senses.

Eating Right

Being mindful of your diet and eating only the foods that serve your body best is the number one way to stay physically clean and clear. This varies from person to person, but in general, the foods I suggest you stay away from are the ones you're probably trying to avoid anyway, processed foods like cookies, muffins, potato chips—really anything made with white flour or white sugar. Heavy dairy products can also clog your system, limiting your ability to see clearly. The same goes for caffeine, drugs, alcohol, and cigarettes.

Are you someone who indulges in a double espresso every afternoon? A candy bar from the vending machine? It's a tempting pick-me-up, but caffeine and sugar will often work against you spiritually because of their racey and anxiety-producing effects. When your mind is going sixty miles per hour, it's hard to be present. Alcohol, on the other hand, works against you in a different way by dulling and shutting down your energy system.

Aim for a fresh diet that allows your body and energy system to remain light, open, and free. For some of you, detoxing or even fasting (cutting out certain foods for a period of time) can be a great thing to do once or twice a year to cleanse and clear toxins and impurities out of your system. Is this for everyone? *No.* (And be sure to consult with your doctor before attempting any detox diet.) Again, listen to your body—it will tell you what it needs.

Get Physical

In addition to watching your diet, find ways to stay physically active. When we don't make time to stretch and move our bodies, we compromise our health and block our intuitive channels because we're stressed and irritable. The less stress we hold in our bodies, the more we free our minds up to sense the higher and subtler energies of Spirit. Choose a physical activity you enjoy and incorporate it into your daily routine. Run, walk, cycle, swim, take a weight-training class, sign up for yoga, dust off your dancing shoes, or join an organized sport like softball, volleyball, or adult kickball. The more you engage your physical body, the higher and deeper your intuitive connections will be. That said, an overly athletic lifestyle can work against us as well. (I know, we can *never* win!) Extremely active people need to be mindful to stretch and relax stressed and fatigued muscles. When our bodies are tense and our muscles aren't allowed to repair, our energy can become blocked. To combat this, massage and other forms of bodywork (chiropractic, energy healing, Reiki, acupuncture) allow us to release tension, toxins, and imbalances.

Another great way to relax our bodies and clear our energy is by soaking in a bath sprinkled with sea salt. It's a simple yet effective way to melt away something that may be standing between us and our ability to connect intuitively and spiritually. Simply fill a tub with warm water and add a cup or so of kosher sea salt and soak in it for a minimum of fifteen minutes. Not only does this relax our fatigued muscles, it opens up our intuitive mind.

Love Your Body

Taking care of your body also means loving your body. If you're ingesting toxic food and substances, avoiding the doctor's office or the gym, check in and ask yourself, *What's this all about? Why aren't I caring for myself?* Do your simple breathing exercise, meditate, and try to get to the root issue—this is important. When I was suffering from depression at the hands of the Night Prowler, I saw my body as a prison. I had no love for my body. In fact, I loathed it, regarded it as the enemy (like it was separate and not part of me), and found myself constantly in battle with it. If you're someone who feels similarly trapped in your own body, know that you're not alone and that you're probably more normal than you realize. I've met hundreds of women who feel this way, so, if that's you—own those feelings and then set the intention to shift them into feelings of honor and love.

> **AFFIRMATION**
>
> *I am transforming negativity about my body into feelings of respect.*

When we're struggling to zip up our skinny jeans or fit back into our pre-baby clothes, it's hard to regard our bodies as a gift given to us to experience the physical world. But it's true. And if we want to stick around and experience life on Earth, we have to take care of the vehicle that's driving us around. It's funny . . . when we're pregnant, we go to great lengths to eat healthy and nutritious foods and avoid certain others for the well-being of the baby growing inside of us. But why don't we do this for ourselves all the time? It should be our daily and lifelong intention to love and care for our bodies. To acknowledge and show gratitude for how hard our bodies work for us every moment of every day, try the My Body Is My Temple meditation on page 240 at the back of the book.

SPIRITUAL WORK

As you continue to tackle your mental, emotional, and physical work, I want you to add in the spiritual component—the most important for allowing intuitive clarity to flow without interruption. Before I go any further, let me give you warning: I'm going to get a little "woo-woo" on you now. (You knew this was coming!) But since you've stuck with me this far, chances are you've become a little woo-woo along the way, too! I'm confident you can handle what's next, and if any of my new-age terminology isn't to your liking, then just make up your own words. *Deal?*

Are You Blocked?

In addition to quieting the mind, the goal of meditation is to connect to our energy and spiritual centers, open them up, and give them a super charge. When these centers are clear and open, it makes it easier for us to receive or pick up intuitive and spiritual messages in our everyday life. Additionally, when our energy centers are open, *life* opens up for us. The right people, auspicious situations, and positive opportunities start flowing our way.

Your body has seven energy centers, or *chakras*, that support your core and run along a central column from the crown of your head to the base of your spine. Your energy centers influence your health greatly. When your energy is unbalanced or gets blocked, you can become very sick. (All disease, whether emotional, mental, or physical, first starts energetically before it manifests physically.) A poor diet, stimulants like coffee and sugar, depressants like alcohol, and a lack of exercise can all act as culprits. Your thoughts and actions also play a part in the health of your energy centers, which is why you must pay attention to the energy you project out into the world as equally as the energy you allow in.

Energy to be wary of:

1) Fear-based ego thoughts (anger, spite, jealousy, resentment) about yourself and others.

2) Spiritually unhealthy or toxic environments—any space that leaves you feeling exhausted, depleted, and yucky.

3) Spiritually unhealthy and toxic people. As discussed earlier, psychic vampires will latch onto your energy unless you protect yourself.

When our energy centers get clogged with negative debris, we're left feeling sluggish, pessimistic, or sick without even knowing why. These feelings are an indication that one or more of our energy centers are out of balance and in need of healing. When our energy centers are cleared and balanced, we feel more alive, positive, and joyful.

To keep your spiritual channels open, I suggest you use the Energy Clearing and Balancing meditation on page 241 in the back of the book. In fact, I urge you do it daily (or at least a version of it, even if you only spend a total of five minutes in meditation). Making this a regular practice will keep you in complete alignment with your highest self, increase your intuitive knowing, and significantly increase the likelihood that you'll connect with higher spiritual energies. It may sound like a lot, but doing this daily doesn't mean you have to rearrange your life. Like anything, if you make it a priority, you'll find the time to do it. Before long, it will become a habit, like going to the gym, making dinner, or watching your favorite TV show.

MAKE A CONNECTION

Now, making contact! In Chapter Five: Tap the Source, I supplied
you with a list of the many ways that Spirit attempts to communicate
with us. Below is a list of ways and places in which *we* can make the first
move to connect with Spirit on a regular basis outside of meditation.

Candles

When our lives turn dark because we've lost someone we love, lost a loving
relationship, or lost our sense of purpose in the world, we may feel compelled to burn candles to bring in light. Spirit can easily connect with the
glowing light of candles, since fire has a similar high vibration, and may
use its energy to manipulate the flame or blow it out as a sign of its presence. Candle lighting ceremonies are a wonderful way to honor Spirit.

Cars

Many of us find our cars to be good places for personal reflection because of the daily "alone time" we spend commuting around town and
sitting in traffic. The act of driving, when not stressful and confronta-
tional, can be a good opportunity to quiet your mind and to pick up a
distinct message from the radio, on a billboard, on a license plate ahead.
In other words, look *both* ways when driving!

Cemeteries and Memorial Sites

The burial or memorial sites of deceased loved ones can be great places
to connect with their energy, not because their spirits reside there—

because they probably don't—but because they can be peaceful meeting grounds free from outside distractions.

True Stories: Memorial Sites

I was once doing a phone reading with a client in another state and I had no idea where she was physically seated when I began the reading. Her husband immediately came through in spirit, thanking her for the yellow roses she recently put at his grave. She gasped and told me she was in fact sitting at his grave right then! She'd just laid down a dozen yellow roses prior to our session. He went on to tell her that she didn't need to be at the grave to "talk" to him. He was with her wherever she sat quietly with the heartfelt intention to connect to his energy.

Houseplants

Plants emit a high vibration and help to clear our living space of negative or fear-based energy. It's a good idea to put a plant close by our beds so they cleanse and balance our energy while we sleep. Spirits are often drawn to the higher energy of plants and may help the plant grow in extreme and unusual ways in an effort to capture our attention.

Meditation

I think I've made this point loud and clear, but I'm sneaking it onto this list one more time to say again—meditate, meditate, meditate.

Music

Music often has a powerful effect on our spiritual energy. It can calm, inspire, and uplift us. It takes us out of our left analytical brain and puts us into our right intuitive and creative brain. Take five minutes and listen to a piece of music that particularly speaks to you. Don't use this as an opportunity to multitask, but as an excuse to slow down and connect with your higher self and with Spirit.

Nature

Getting out into the fresh air within a natural setting grounds us in our bodies and clears our stagnant energy. Being out in sunlight separates us from the material world and helps to remind us that we are spiritual beings. Whether we're sitting in a park, daydreaming in our backyard, hiking in the mountains, or walking along the beach, our minds are more likely to be in the present moment and invite Spirit to connect with us.

Ouija and Angel Boards

A Ouija or angel board is often used as a game. It consists of a board and planchette that is moved around by Spirit to get answers to questions. This can open the door to dark entities if you're not well grounded or clear on your purpose or intention, so be careful and take the necessary steps to avoid any negative experience. This can be as simple as offering a prayer of protection and setting the intention that only loving and positive energy come through. Remember, we are always in control of our experience and what we let into our lives. When the board is used for healing and loving guidance and communication, it can serve as an effective and powerful tool.

Pendulum

This is a simple tool consisting of a string or chain with a weighted object suspended on one end. The purpose of the pendulum is to amplify the energy around one's physical body in order to receive insight into one's health (physical, mental, or emotional) in a process called pendulum dowsing or pendulum divining. Some people say that the pendulum creates a bridge between the logical and intuitive parts of the mind. How does it work? Just as radios pick up information from unseen radio waves, the pendulum can be a powerful antenna that receives information from the vibrations and energy waves emitted by people, places, thoughts, and things. Research by many scientists indicates that the pendulum responds to electromagnetic energy that radiates from everything on the planet.

Prayer

While meditation is us *listening* to God, Spirit, and our intuitive knowing, prayer is when we *talk* to God and to Spirit. How do we *talk* to Spirit? The key is asking Spirit to intervene (remember: they need an invitation) and then believing you will receive guidance. It may feel like a one-sided conversation at first, but when we pray, either mentally or aloud, and ask for strength, help, or advice, we will start to witness how Spirit moves through and assists us in our lives.

Redecorate and Clean

A cluttered and unorganized home is often a reflection of a cluttered mind, so cleaning our home and office space can be helpful to our mental state. In addition to simply tidying up, I suggest painting the walls with fresh paint, cleaning or replacing the carpeting, changing out old furniture, and giving away items we no longer use. These are great ways to shift energy in the home—creating a space that feels light and open to clear thinking.

Space Clearing

It's important to clean our environments of toxic energy. Just as holding on to old possessions can weigh us down and create a block in the flow, there's a great deal of energy that gets soaked up and trapped in our walls, floors, and furniture. When the energy is negative, over time it builds and feels uncomfortable to be around. It may be from you, other people living in the space, or former owners or occupants of the property. There are many ways to clear the space (sage smudging is one example) so that the energy is lighter, more positive and loving, allowing for more connection with spirit energy.

Spirit Symbolism

The only way to learn your own symbolism is to first make a date with your spirit guides. Tell them, *I am ready for you to show me how you are going to communicate with me.* It may sound a little direct, but this is exactly what I did. Early on in my work, they were showing me three different symbols for yes: sunshine, a smile, and a green light. I needed clarity, so I said, show me the ONE symbol that you will use for yes, and a green light appeared in my mind. From that day on, when I see a green light, I know *exactly* what it means. Now of course that doesn't mean *your* symbol for yes will be the same. As I explained before, Spirit will use your individual frame of reference to communicate with you. The key is to be patient and remain flexible while you develop and learn your symbolism. Don't force it—just stop and pay attention and it will come.

Spiritual Study

When we open ourselves up to exploring our spiritual understanding and knowledge, we automatically begin to shift our energy to the higher frequency of Spirit. Each of us will connect to different spiritual material and it doesn't matter what path or spiritual affiliation one chooses to follow. I believe that spiritual study is an effective way to help each of us find deeper meaning and connection to our inner self throughout our lifetime.

Trips

When we step into unfamiliar territory, either by taking a vacation or traveling for work, we tend to be more present and in tune with our intuition. Everything is new and our senses are heightened. It's often in these times when our mind is open and more relaxed that we will connect with spirit energy and experience clarity.

Water

Water is a powerful element that makes up 60 percent of our bodies, so we're naturally drawn to it. When we're separated from water for long periods of time we may experience mood swings or controlling tendencies, or become self-indulgent. Being around water assists in our energy flow, making us more open, centered, calm, and connected to our intuition and to spirit energy. Take the salt bath I mentioned earlier.

The Power of Prayer

After having lived in Santa Monica, CA, for less than three years, I started having dreams that it was time for us to pack up and move once again. I struggled with the guidance because it made no sense. *Why did we have to move again?* I prayed and prayed over the information and one morning in particular, I asked my guides for one direct and clear sign that I could not deny. *If I get a sign,* I told myself, *I will honor the guidance and have the courage to follow through with it.* About an hour later, Brian asked me to go for a walk with him, and about five minutes into the walk, I saw a blank 3x5 index card with black writing on the ground. I bent down to pick it up and on it read in big bold letters, "YES, MOVE." *Truly I'm not making this up.*

I had my clear sign (no question!) and was once again in awe of how Spirit works for us. As much as we loved and enjoyed our time in California, we packed up, trusting all the dots would continue to connect as we followed our guidance. We moved just a few months later.

THE IMPORTANCE OF DOING THE WORK

The purpose of this chapter is to help you become aware of your mental, emotional, physical, and spiritual energy. The energy you put out into the world directly affects your life experience. Therefore, we can design and create the lives we've always wanted for ourselves. While this should come as exciting news, it also means *no more excuses*! If we're not happy with the reality we're waking up to in the morning, it's our responsibility to change it. We can redirect our lives by making the best choices for ourselves from *this moment on*. This is what "doing the work" is all about. With vigilant effort, good things are on the way for you.

After the birth of my second son, I started to slip into postpartum depression. I found myself crying on and off throughout the day, feeling sad, irritable, and negative. I barely recognized myself. I hadn't felt that low since my Night Prowler days and that was my wake-up call. Because I'd been in that dark, scary place before, I knew it was important to address it pronto instead of ignoring it. So, I went to my nutritionist and chiropractor, who use alternative healing methods, and they both agreed I should get some blood work done. Turns out I have a low-functioning thyroid, a very low vitamin D level, and very low progesterone levels—a recipe for BIGTIME depression. After learning this, I was on it! I started taking supplements and vitamins to bring me back into balance. I got myself to the gym and on a healthy diet. I spent a ridiculous amount of time in meditation and I journaled about the whole process. Through it all, I wondered, *If Grandma Babe had done the work, would her life have turned out differently?*

You Always Have a Choice

As I know I've drilled into you, you can wake up and do the work now, in this life, or you can choose to do it later in the afterlife. Either way, you have to do the work. My grandmother Babe is a perfect example of this. She suffered from severe postpartum depression and she never dealt with it effectively; over several decades, it grew into this demon that eventually led to her suicide. As I've said, her suicide was not an effective means of escaping her pain.

Like it was with Grandma Babe, spirits who hurt you in the past or had similar challenges often become your spirit guides to help you learn, heal, and break a destructive chain. If you give them permission to work with you, you also give them an opportunity to heal and evolve themselves.

SHELLY'S STORY

I want to finish this chapter by sharing my father's story with you. My dad, Babe's son, Shelly Perelman, is the one who ingrained in me one of my favorite mantras: *There's no magic pill. You've got to do the work!*

In Chapter One: Is This Woman for Real?, I explained that my father tried to commit suicide the first semester I was off at college. In the ten years that followed, Dad did a great deal of soul searching. He became an avid spiritual seeker and teacher who wholeheartedly believed that our souls are eternal. He was doing the work, and as a result, he was growing and evolving. But while he was spiritually connected and aware, Dad still struggled with his meddlesome mind thoughts. He was haunted by his mother's suicide and his guilt. He blamed himself for her death and he struggled with self-love and self-worth issues. All of this pain and heartache resurfaced as he dug deeper into his soul and spirituality. This created a great internal divide between his mind and his soul. As a result, he eventually fell back into a deep depression.

My father wrongfully thought that it was unholy or "unspiritual" to need medication for his depression. He wanted to believe that his awakened spirituality was enough to keep him on track, that drugs would block him somehow. What I've come to learn is that if you're someone who needs medication to get balanced, drugs may actually *help* you become more present to connect with Spirit. (The truth is, some people are chemically imbalanced and need regular, prescribed medication to keep them in a good place, while others use medicine as a quick fix incorrectly. In any case, it's very important to work with professionals to determine what your specific needs are.) When my father, who was absolutely chemically imbalanced, refused medication, he eventually withdrew back into his "shell." In a moment of great despair and darkness, he decided to end his pain. On October 17, 2006, in his Birmingham, Michigan, home, he killed himself.

My dad himself always said that "everything is a gift; every experience that we encounter along our journey is an opportunity to grow if we choose to see it that way." After several months of agonizing pain and grief following my father's death, I decided to look for the silver lining. It wasn't easy, but gradually the dark legacy of suicide in my family crystallized in my mind my knowing of *why* God has blessed me with this divine gift. My father's death inspired me to push forward with my life's work as a medium, healer, and spiritual teacher to awaken and encourage us to take full responsibility for our unresolved issues, and to heal our wounds in *this* lifetime.

I candidly share my father's story, as I have been guided to do. He often visits me in my dreams, and on more than one occasion, he has shared with me the deep regret and sadness he now faces for his irreversible act . . . Now that he is free of his human mind, he can see clearly that he was imbalanced and in great need of professional help. He's currently in a healing energy, much like a hospital ICU, to reflect, restore, and eventually revisit and redo his lessons in order to balance out his negative karma.

I know he would want nothing more than to serve as a reminder of all these truths that he preached, but struggled to integrate into his physical experience. If you (or someone you know) happen to find yourself traveling down a similar road of depression, I hope that my father's story will awaken your mind and heart to the knowledge that you don't have to wait until you return to Spirit to live in freedom, peace, and love.

I pray that every moment I show up to do healing work, both personally and professionally, that I redeem both my grandmother's and father's wounded spirits, and bring a smile to their resting souls.

7

✳

Let Go

If you've gotten to the heart of your struggle, then you've gotten yourself on the right path. And if you've gotten into the routine of doing your work, in some ways there's nothing more to learn. So, it's time to get out of your own way and let your life unfold! In this final chapter, I'll walk you through:

- The importance of moving forward,
- The purpose of your life,
- A glimpse of the bigger picture, and
- How to let go and live your life!

KEEP MOVING FORWARD

The recent and tragic loss of my dad brought me face to face with the deep pain that many of my clients experience after losing a loved one. Still, after confronting the enormity of it, I knew I had to march on in order to keep up with my life. I knew Dad would want me to continue doing my work. But grief and heartache are powerful emotions, and there were many days when I really struggled to do the simplest things—make breakfast for my son, blow-dry my hair, drive to work. I was grateful that I had family responsibilities and a job that I needed to show up for—these tasks kept me focused when it would have been so easy to sink into the dark corner of my sadness.

After several months of intense professional work, I took several days off with the intention to begin writing this book. Spirit had been tapping me on the shoulder to do so. The idea came up in meditation and began popping into my mind at random times, like when I was at the gas station. So, on my first free morning off from work, I woke up, sat down at the computer and . . . nothing. I intuitively felt a strong sense that it was time, but my mind was resisting. All I wanted to do was watch mindless television or go back to bed. But I didn't. I sat in front of my computer, and sat, and sat. After wasting an hour wrestling with my mind over *what to write . . . should I write . . . do I even know how to write?* I decided to get out of the house and clear my mind. Maybe if I went to a bookstore, it would inspire me?

I got in the car and headed to my local Barnes and Noble. As I started to drive, I was immediately flooded with gratitude for my life's work as a medium. I realized why the guidance for writing a book had been relentless and strong. God has blessed me with a gift that proves to me that, despite how dark it may get, everything is in perfect order. It may sound strange to call my father's suicide a gift, but it was indeed an inspiration to work on my own stuff and to continue my work as a medium, to help others.

As I continued to drive, I knew my strong thoughts and feelings were being inspired by my spirit guides, but just to bring the point home—a car suddenly pulled in front of me, nearly cutting me off. My eyes locked on the license plate that read: "WRITE2!" I gasped. *You've got to be kidding me!* My eyes filled with tears at the incredible validation. Not only was the Universe confirming my intuitive gift, but it was giving me the nudge I needed—*Write that book already!*

THE PURPOSE OF YOUR LIFE

Our ultimate goal is to live a life of integrity and love that helps raise the consciousness of the planet. *But no pressure.* OKAY, let me phrase it another way. Our goal is to reach our highest potential and the highest expression of ourselves. So, how do we do that? The answer is, whatever we do, DO IT WITH LOVE. You can be a teacher, a health-care professional, a stay-at-home mom, an artist—it doesn't matter *what* you do. It only matters that you do it with love. When our actions, words, and thoughts are kind, gentle, gracious, and loving, that's when we're being the highest expression of ourselves. We really can't go any higher than that.

> **AFFIRMATION**
>
> *I open my heart and allow myself to receive and send love.*

We all tend to confuse purpose with talent. They aren't the same thing. For example, you may be a *talented* cook who became a great chef. Well, just because you're naturally exceptional in the kitchen doesn't necessarily mean that cooking is your purpose in life. Your purpose is to be the highest expression of yourself, which is love. If you express your love through your cooking, well then, you're indeed fulfilling your purpose. See the difference?

Take Steven Spielberg, for instance. What would you say his purpose in life is? He's an exceptionally talented and gifted filmmaker, no? He's made countless films that have impacted the world in a positive way. He's used his influence and celebrity to expose and help heal social wounds caused by the Holocaust, slavery, and terrorism. It would seem that his God-given purpose is to be a filmmaker. But I'd argue that his purpose is to be the highest expression of himself, which is to serve others and be a loving spirit, which he just so happens to express beautifully through his films. Our work is only a vehicle for our love.

Ultimately, we're here to spiritually evolve and we do this by serving

Prayer for My Highest Self to Shine Through

At night before I go to bed, I say a prayer . . . *Bless my family and friends and all those people in need of comfort, healing, and love. I* recite what I'm grateful for and ask to be renewed in my sleep with the help of my guides and angels. I ask to be cleansed of any fear that I may have picked up throughout the day and to be brought back to a place of love and faith.

others, in big ways and small. When we each embrace our unique and special talents to do service, we help heal the energy of the planet. Every time I do a reading for someone, I keep this in mind: *This isn't just an "ability"—it's my purpose.*

Again, it's not important what work you do. Titles really mean nothing. We're drawn to different paths based on what our soul needs to learn. None is better or worse, or more or less important than another. So, try not to compete or compare yourself with others. Instead, open up and allow your own gifts to organically evolve. God has blessed each and every one of us with unique talents that we can share by doing nothing more than being who we already are. How easy is that?

THE BIGGER PICTURE

Somehow, we've gotten all the way to the end of the book without getting into a deep discussion about *what happens when we die.* Well, better late than never! In the workshops I lead, this is a question that always comes up, so I'm assuming it's crossed your mind at least a few times throughout these pages.

After working with spirit energy over the past decade, my understanding of death is that it's as individual and unique as our experiences in life. That said, many of our popular beliefs and ideas about death appear to be not too far off the mark. A tunnel, flashes of light, final judgment—it turns out that Hollywood's version of "The End" is pretty realistic.

Spirits regularly impress me with thoughts and feelings of going through a tunnel, seeing a bright light, meeting up with passed loved ones, and hanging out in some sort of waiting room. Many describe a blissful and magical feeling where they're absolutely exhilarated to "go home," with no desire to turn around and come back. The even bigger *Aha!* is the realization that although our physical bodies die, our consciousness lives on. What does this mean? It means you finally get to say, *I am so much more than my body!* At this point in the death experience, one of two things will happen: 1) If it's our time to go, we let go and cross over. 2) If it isn't our time to go, our spirits come back into our bodies so we can finish our business on Earth.

Hold On! I Don't Get It: Who or *what* decides if it's our "time to go"?

Here's the Deal: The timing of our deaths may seem arbitrary and unfair, but it's really not. The truth is, each one of us has already chosen our own death. That's right, YOU chose it. Remember back in Chapter Three: What's Your Damage? when I explained how you, along with your spirit group and guides, determined the lessons you needed to learn in this lifetime? Well, you also scripted a few possible exit points before coming into this life. (Of course, we have no knowing of this on a conscious level. This information would only serve to work against us. Too much information is just that—*too much*. We come into this life with a form of amnesia, so that we can be present and not distracted by our past.)

It's "our time" if we have reached the point where we've learned all we were meant to learn in this lifetime for our soul's growth. *But you said we don't always learn all our lessons before we die!* Good catch! What I've heard from Spirit is that when we incarnate, we don't set out to learn it ALL in one go around. We line up a specific amount of key things to work on, and have high hopes of accomplishing as much as possible. I like to think of it this way: We're all at different spots on the same yellow brick road, so the challenges and lessons we each need to learn are different. (You might be fighting off flying monkeys while I'm still searching for the courage to go into battle.) The truth is: It takes some souls several lifetimes to learn one simple lesson, like overcoming greed or learning self-love. When our time comes, we decide if we've done our best and have done enough. If the answer is *yes*, we go home. If it's *no*, we may choose to stick around a while longer. This is often how near-death experiences can be explained: We reach our exit point and realize there's still work to be done, so we come back into our body with the resolve to do the work. You've probably heard of people who, after nearly dying, regain consciousness with a new and joyful lease on life. They hop back on the yellow brick road and start skipping ahead.

What This Means for You: Don't be afraid of death. It's going to happen, and when it does, have faith in knowing that your life is unfolding just as it was meant to—just as YOU set it up to unfold.

Hold On! I Still Don't Get It: So, are you saying that someone who suffers a painful death has chosen this? And what about the *really* bad endings?

Here's the Deal: Everyone dies differently depending on what they need to learn, or what we can help those around us learn. For example, some die slowly, and suffer a long good-bye because they still need to learn how to receive love and care from others, and in their hospitalized state they can finally surrender and accept love. In other cases, people hang on because their family members won't let them go. I hear this all the time in readings—it's often the living who have the harder time allowing the dying to die. In the instance of a sudden or tragic death like a car accident or a murder, the soul, or spirit, will almost always immediately eject and disassociate from the body to avoid pain. Sometimes, a spirit will stay in its body if it has something to gain or learn from the pain.

A spirit usually detaches and hovers over its physical body until it dies. In readings, Spirit has described floating above the body, attached by a silver cord until death cuts them free. Spirit has also described drifting up and away from the body and going straight into the light. Some of my clients who have watched their loved ones die have confirmed this vision. They describe a light lifting out of the body and then flying around the room like a little Tinker Bell.

What This Means for You: Try to stop associating death with pain. And know that your physical death isn't the end for you. You don't disappear—you just change form and continue living, like water evaporating and returning to the sky.

Now to answer your question—I promise I'm not avoiding it—what about when really bad things happen to good people? This comes up in my group readings all the time. People want to know, "What about tragic events? How do you make sense out of horrible things?" While I can't offer the comfort that many of these people need and desire, I can share my unique perspective. Spirit has taught me that bad events fall into one of two categories: group exit points and random acts of chaos.

A group exit point is where a group of beings agree on a soul level before they're born into their physical bodies to exit life at the same time to teach an important lesson. Often a tragic event like a natural disaster brings out the goodness or "godliness" in humankind, giving us, the collective, an opportunity to evolve on a larger soul level. This is part of the "big" work I mentioned at the beginning of the chapter.

For grieving individuals and families who have lost someone in such a way, this can be a difficult concept to swallow. I completely understand that. *Why did my daughter . . . my son . . . my wife have to die?* As devastating and impossible to justify as it may be, the event itself is not necessarily random. Spirits often sign up ahead of time to sacrifice their lives so a great lesson can be learned.

True Stories: Tragic Event

A married couple once came to me for a reading because they were completely broken up over the death of their young boy. Their son drowned in their backyard pool and they were in the process of suing the pool manufacturer over his death. As anyone would be, they were devastated, angry, and vengeful.

Not minutes into the reading, their son in spirit came through. He assured his mother and father that he died at the right time and he urged them not to blame anyone for his death. If he hadn't drowned, he relayed to me, he would have gone some other way and just as soon. His young death was inevitable because he had "contracted" to live for only five or six years. He had agreed to cross over at that point and act as a spirit guide for his brother and sister. Guiding his siblings through life was his purpose. As hard as it was for this couple to hear this, they thanked me and said they felt relief for the first time since his death.

When we're able to catch a glimpse of the bigger picture and see our lives through what I like to call "God's eyes," we can feel gratitude knowing that everything is happening as it should and that every experience (even the most horrible obstacles) provides us with an opportunity to spiritually grow.

A random act of chaos, on the other hand, is a very different story. Some tragic events aren't necessarily intended to happen for the greater good. In situations like Waco and Columbine, for example, evil people have used the power of their own free wills to carry out horrendous acts on innocent people. Still, those bystanders or victims have somehow attracted themselves to the scene or situation because their energy is a match to the chaotic energy of the event. Does that mean they "deserved" to die? No, not at all. People often ask me, *Rebecca, do you believe in evil?* The answer is yes: I believe we are all capable of evil, just as we are capable of absolute goodness. I regard evil as the *lack of* goodness, or lack of godliness. I do not see evil as a separate entity. There is good and then there is the lack of good, just as darkness is the lack of light. Darkness is not its own force. Those who do evil are those who have fallen off track—they're disconnected from themselves and their own godliness.

Everything holds a certain vibrational frequency—people, places, objects, etc. Through the Law of Attraction, our vibration (or energy) will attract like vibrations to us. So, when we have habitual thoughts and feelings like *I expect that bad things will happen to me,* we unconsciously attract bad things to come our way. This is why it absolutely pays off to think positively, as I've explained, and to only project the kind of energy you want to get back.

✦ TESTIMONIAL

On August 31, 2002, I lost my eldest child, Jason. His death was unanticipated, and untimely as Jason was a vibrant twenty-five-year-old young man. My husband, Michael, and I were enjoying the beginning of Labor Day weekend. However, something felt awry that Saturday. Usually my husband spoke with Jason several times daily. When we called Jason that Saturday morning and received his voice mail message . . . we didn't really think twice. However, as the morning progressed to early afternoon we became concerned. Our concerns grew after we received a call from the barber who said that Jason missed his haircut appointment. Again, not believing that such a trag-edy awaited us, yet being concerned parents, we decided to stop by Jason's apartment. My husband discovered Jason. Weeks later, we learned that Jason suffered from heart failure.

I was dreading November 4, 2002—Jason's twenty-sixth birthday. November 4th was also the last session in a series of Rebecca Rosen's seminars. My friends were at a loss for how to help me through this day. They decided to take me to Rebecca's seminar that evening. What followed turned a day of despair into a day of new beliefs.

I came to the seminar skeptical, but in my heart I was hopeful that somehow, some way, Jason would deliver some kind of message. Dur-ing the first half of the seminar, I was an audience member, just like everyone else. Things quickly changed prior to the intermission when Rebecca reached out to the audience to announce that a mother was in the audience who suddenly and recently lost a son. This lost son had been with Rebecca all day with desperate hopes of reaching his mother that evening.

My heart was pounding with anticipation. Somehow I knew that Rebecca was talking about me. Following the intermission, Rebecca started to approach me. She was speaking quite rapidly, and with such stunning accuracy that it brought me to tears. She gave me Jason's name, the date of his death, and the fact that there was no time for "good-bye's." The following is Jason's message through Rebecca:

Jason spoke of his brother, "Jeffrey," his best friend, "Bradley," his father, and me. He acknowledged that November 4th was his birth-day, and he was blowing me kisses. He also wanted to send love to his girlfriend. He was desperate to let us know that he was okay, and that he was still with us. He also wanted us to know that he was not alone. Jason was also able to recount through Rebecca uncanny de-tails of our daily lives since his passing. Specifically, Jason was laugh-ing over my recent fetish with arranging and rearranging photos of him. Jason was also aware of a trip to Las Vegas that we had just arranged only three days prior. You see, this trip was to celebrate Jason's younger brother, Jeff's twenty-first birthday. We had done the same for Jason only five years earlier. He assured us that he would be with us on this trip.

This day, November 4th, changed my view on life and the afterlife forever. I am no longer a skeptic. I believe in connections beyond the physical presence. I am a mother who still aches every moment of every day for the physical loss of her child. But at least I can now believe that someday we will reconnect in the spiritual world. I thank Rebecca Rosen for being able to serve as a bridge between me and my son, Jason.

Jackie from Novi, Michigan

There's no greater joy than being able to offer people tangible evidence of life after death, giving them hope and renewed faith after grieving the loss of a loved one. I seem to have a knack for attracting the spirits of children, teens, and young adults that have passed away. I believe one of the most devastating losses is that of a child, so when I get to make a connection between a lost child and his or her parents, I feel such immense gratitude and appreciation for my gift. Instances like this perfectly illustrate *why* I do what I do. One never "gets over" the death of a loved one, but we can learn to appreciate a new normal, and develop a new relationship with the spirit of someone we loved.

THE OTHER SIDE

Once on the "other side," we each spend time reviewing our lives—the lessons we learned, where we went right, where we went wrong. Depending on how you lived your life, you'll either be promoted to a higher level of spiritual evolution, or you won't. Now being promoted isn't contingent on having a pristine and perfect record. (Thank goodness!) We all make mistakes—that's a given. Making positive progress on a soul level isn't about being flawless, but about the progress we made in regard to the *intentions* we set in life to be good and better people. Who sits in judgment on this? *You* do. Let me explain . . .

According to Spirit, we go through a sort of exit interview process, where we sit in counsel initially with our spirit guides and later with our soul group and review the contract we made with ourselves before we incarnated into our physical body. That's when it's truth time and we have to answer the questions: *Did I follow my script? Did I learn the lessons that I set up for myself in order to evolve on a soul level? Did I pass my own tests?* We take an inventory of the life we lived, and determine what work we need to do in spirit form to heal and recover and prepare a new contract for what we need to learn in our *next* lifetime.

Hold On! I Don't Get It: Are you saying that if I totally screw up, it doesn't really count because I can just come back and fix it the next time around?

Here's the Deal: No, everything counts.

What This Means for You: If you really screw up, you'll have to start back at square one. Think of it this way—you make it all the way to your senior year of high school, and then you mess up and fail all your classes. Instead of having to repeat your senior year before you can graduate (which would suck), you have to go *all* the way back to kindergarten and start from scratch. *Doesn't sound like much fun, does it?* Moral of the story: keep your mess-ups to a minimum.

I once did a reading for a woman over the phone, and immediately her mother came through, expressing concern for her daughter's well-being. She impressed upon me that her daughter was in an unhappy marriage, and that it was time to put an end to the emotional and mental abuse from her husband. Her mother's spirit showed me a bottle of pills and so I asked my client if she was suicidal. When my client heard this, she broke down crying, admitting that she had the pills sitting right next to her and was waiting until after the reading to make the decision whether to take them. Her mother clearly expressed for her daughter not to commit suicide, as she'd just be running away from a big life lesson of standing up for herself, and her baggage would follow her into the afterlife. She wouldn't beat the system. She'd have to start all over again.

THOSE SOULS WHO need lots of healing and recovery (the mentally ill and those who have taken their own lives, as well as those who did evil acts or caused harm to others) are taken to a place where they are cocooned in intense healing energy to restore their depleted spirit. The rest of us who aren't in such dire need of healing gravitate to the spiritual level that corresponds with our energy, or vibration. The level we ascend to depends on our thoughts, words, and deeds while on Earth (yes, Karma is a bitch!). Our addictions, unhealthy behavior, and negative thoughts follow us into the spiritual realm and when we review our lives, it becomes strikingly clear why we should have let those habits go—they block our spiritual growth.

Think of spiritual growth and evolution from a scale of one to ten. The lowest level (number one) is what many of you call "Hell," which isn't really a place, but a state of mind where we're disconnected from ourselves and separated from Source. Hell is the absence of light and love, and it's created by negative thoughts and behavior. Anyone filled with hate and darkness resides here and will stay in this self-created dark hole until the soul chooses otherwise. The sooner the soul can let go of the fear-driven ego, the faster it can lighten, brighten, and grow.

The Book of Life

f you're curious about reviewing all of your lifetimes and how they played out, you may want to look them up in the Akashic records. Ever heard of 'em? Unfortunately, you can't find them in your nearest library. They are housed in the astral plane and are thought to contain the records of all human knowledge and history. Crazy, right? While accessing the memory of the Universe is no simple thing, reading up on this mysterious subject matter is. Next time you're on Amazon.com, look up "Akashic records" and you'll see what I mean.

THE HIGH LIFE

Once our spirit is ready to ditch self-destructive habits, behaviors, and thoughts, we go through another death, which allows our spirit to advance to a higher level. The higher we go, the closer we get to Heaven (number ten on the scale), a place of oneness and inner peace where spiritual beings blend into one divine light.

After spending a while soaking up the light of Source and filling up on oneness and spiritual love, a spirit may decide to reenter the dense conditions of the physical world, referred to as *reincarnation*. On average, a soul waits about two generations (one hundred years or so) before returning to a body, and does so either to inspire others with the insights and knowledge gained in the spiritual realm or to master the lessons we can only learn in the classroom called Earth. When our spirit returns to a body, we start again where we left off—at the spiritual level we earned (or evolved to) the last time around.

As you continue to do your own work, remember that you're not alone on the field. You've got a squad of spiritual cheerleaders on the sidelines screaming, *GO! GO! GO! You can do it!* When you need their help or encouragement, all you have to do is ask for it. When I'm feeling scattered and disconnected from my intuitive knowing and craving the gentle and calming presence of Spirit, I often do the Meet Your Guides meditation on page 235 or the Over the Rainbow meditation on page 249.

FINALLY, LET GO!

My dad came to me in a dream a couple of weeks ago, telling me it was time for "one last hug." He said he was proud of me for doing the work and encouraged me to continue to take good care of myself and then he was gone. I woke up from the dream with tears in my eyes, feeling his remorse over his suicide, the life lessons he ultimately ignored, and how it was my responsibility to break the cycle of depression in my family. Where Dad and Grandma Babe failed, I must succeed.

Later that day, I went to my energy healer (it's a psychic medium thing) and she immediately started working on my lower back. She said, "You have a tear in your second chakra. It's as if someone ripped out your etheric cord." (Our etheric cord is a band of invisible energy that ties us to people, both living and dead.)

She continued, "I believe it has to do with someone in your family who suffered from deep depression." Then she blurted out, "It's your *dad*! It's as if he's freeing you from carrying his pain and he's allowing you to heal and feel light and happy again!"

I was stunned. But then again, I really wasn't. What she said was total confirmation of my dream. My dad has finally moved on. Since then, I've felt the heavy sadness from his death lift off of me. I haven't felt his presence since then, but I know he's never far away.

As we come to the conclusion of *Spirited*, I want you to promise me that you're not going to throw all your new wisdom away. Your work isn't finished—it's an ongoing process. What you've learned from these pages you can put into practice for the rest of your life. *Right?* Relate it to the same philosophy that many people have about two-week diets—they don't work. But a long-term, well-balanced eating plan does. Eventually, you'll see bigtime results and maintaining the "diet" will become an unconscious lifestyle choice.

Because of my awareness of Spirit and the awakening of my intuition, my life flows easily and effortlessly as long as I stay out of my own way! I never feel alone, I always feel supported and guided, and I know that all I have to do is call upon Spirit for assistance when I need it. I live in love, and not fear. I no longer wake up feeling afraid, inadequate, or doubtful because I know that everything is in divine perfect order. I walk through life *wide awake*, welcoming and honoring the flow. As a result, my life is full of miracles and everyday guidance.

I'm sure you're familiar with the song that goes, "Row, row, row your boat, gently down the stream. Merrily, merrily, merrily, merrily, life is but a dream." This perfectly illustrates the human experience. In the end, it's all but a dream. We're here to do the work (row), go with the flow (gently down the stream), enjoy the ride (merrily), and eventually, each wake up from this dream and remember we agreed to participate in this human experience to spiritually grow and evolve.

Before we end here, take a look at your life. Does it look different than it did seven chapters ago? I hope it does, and I bet it will only continue to change. I mean, there's no way you can go back to your old way of thinking and living because now, *you're* wide awake. You're clear, in the present, feeling intuitively, and connecting with Spirit. And it feels good, doesn't it? This is the first step in your healing. Things will continue to confront and challenge you, but now you have the tools and the support to overcome your obstacles. So, before you say, "Thanks, Rebecca. No offense, but I don't need you anymore. I'll take it from here," let me give you some final words of advice: Be patient, stay open, keep inviting Spirit into your life, and remember, you're powerful beyond measure and you can absolutely have the life you want. Now, go live!

Appendix A

*

Meditation Menu

Easy-Peasy Meditations

Mind Tricks for Those Who Can't Stop Thinking

Get Grounded and Plug In

Let Go and Fill Up

White Light Protection (Psychic Shielding)

Release the Grief and Forgive

Meet Your Guides

Planting the Seeds

Heart Opener

My Body Is My Temple

Tips for making the most of your meditation practice:

1) Set aside time each day, preferably the same time of day, for
yourself to go within and meditate.

2) Create an atmosphere that is relaxing, familiar, and quiet. Lighting candles, burning incense, or diffusing fragrant oils can assist in calming your mind and connecting intuitively.

3) Decide on a comfortable position, either seated with your spine straight and feet planted firmly on the floor, a cross-legged position, or lying down. Close your eyes and relax.

4) Breaths should be slow and deep, breathing in through the nose and exhaling through the mouth.

5) Just allow whatever mind thoughts that come up to pass, and simply return your focus to your breath.

6) Relax in the knowing that you are always in control, and at any point in time you can safely come out of the deep meditative state.

Start Breathing

{THIS SIMPLE BREATHING MEDITATION HELPS TO QUIET THE MIND AND GET PRESENT AND IS THE BASIS FOR THE FOLLOWING MEDITA-TIONS TO BUILD UPON.}

What you'll need: Five undisturbed minutes. Choose a quiet place where you feel comfortable. It doesn't matter where you are, as long as it's an environment that puts you at ease.

Close your eyes and begin to breathe deeply. After a few deep breaths, focus on clearing out your "icky" energy. Take a minute and ask any negative energy that's hanging around to hit the road. Continue to breathe. Notice your breath start to slow down and become a steady flow of inhales and exhales.

For the next five minutes focus on quieting your mind chatter. Release thoughts about yesterday or last week or last year. The goal here is to stop thinking about the past or the future and to learn what it feels like to be fully in the present moment.

Breathe. Let your worries and anxieties drift away. Continue like this for five minutes, or as long as you'd like.

Easy-Peasy Meditations

{DO ANY OF THESE TO SIMPLY QUIET DOWN THE INNER CHITCHAT}

Below is a short list of places to be and activities that I find allow meditation to occur not only more easily, but also more enjoyably. I suggest picking one that suits you and finding a time in the day when you can regularly commit to doing it.

1) **Get outside.** Getting out into the fresh air within a natural setting is an easy and spectacular way to calm the mind. Nature grounds us in our bodies and clears our stagnant energy. Whether you sit in a city park or, your backyard, take a hike, or walk along the beach, your mind is likely to stop the constant chatter and allow you to be in the present moment.

2) **Take a bath.** A great way to clear your toxic energy is by soaking in a bath sprinkled with sea salt or any other natural, aromatic scent that pleases your senses. It is a simple yet effective way to melt away anything that might be standing between you and your ability to connect intuitively. (Salt is known to cleanse negative energy and water often enhances our intuitive ability, especially if you are a water sign.)

3) **Cook.** Cooking is a love and a passion for many people because it can be so therapeutic and creative. If the kitchen is a positive space for you—a place where you allow yourself to relax and quiet your mind—then make this your meditation space. The next time you are preparing a dish, focus on staying present and open to your intuition.

4) **Listen to music.** For many of us, music has a powerful effect on our spiritual energy. It can calm, inspire, and uplift us. It often takes us out of our left analytical brain and puts us into our right intuitive and creative brain. Take five minutes and listen to a piece of music that particularly speaks to you. Don't use this as an opportunity to multitask, but as an excuse to slow down, quiet your mind, and connect with your higher self.

5) **Move.** When we don't make time to open up our bodies and allow energy to move through us, we tend to get blocked, stressed, and irritable. Inactivity affects our physical and mental health, making it difficult for us to connect intuitively. Physical activity, such as walking, running, hiking, cycling, swimming, rollerblading, weight training, and yoga, are excellent ways to stay centered and balanced. I like to do yoga postures to help me stay focused on the present. When my mind starts to drift to my to-do list, my postures weaken and I tumble over.

If none of these meditations works for you, then find something that does work for you and do exactly that! There is no right or wrong here. Use your five minutes of daily meditation time to do whatever it is that allows you to feel safe letting go. More than how you do it, what's most important is your genuine intention to quiet your thoughts. Eventually, your mind will slow down, open up, and make room for a deeper level of awareness.

Mind Tricks for Those Who Can't Stop Thinking

{DO THIS WHEN THE MIND THOUGHTS ARE KEEPING YOU AWAKE. THE FOLLOWING EXERCISES WILL GIVE YOU SOMETHING FOR YOUR MIND TO FOCUS ON, ALLOWING YOU TO PARK IT IN THE PRESENT.}

What you'll need: A comfortable pillow and the lights out!

Lie in bed, close your eyes, and mentally count backward from 100. You may visualize the numbers in your head, or mentally say them. That's not important. What *is* important is that you count each breath, so for example, inhale on 100, exhale on 99, inhale on 98, exhale on 97, and so on and so on. Most likely, you won't get very far into it before you start to drift off to sleep. If your mind wanders between numbers, don't worry about it. Return to your number count as soon as you recognize it.

Choose a word or mantra that speaks to you, and mentally repeat it over and over. I have two favorite, simple mantras: *Just be* and *Let go, let God*. Sometimes I repeat my mantra when I'm having a difficult time clearing my mind or getting to sleep. I mentally repeat my mantra over and over (maybe for fifteen or more minutes) until I start to receive intuitive insights, spiritual connections, or simply nod off.

Place a notepad and pen next to your bed and when your mind starts racing, write everything down. Unload your thoughts on paper and get them off and out of the mind. This could be to-do lists, grocery lists, appointment reminders, plans for the future, unsettled feelings, or ideas for a project. When I unload and write it down in my notebook, I'm able to fall back asleep knowing that I've made a list and can tackle it in the morning, but for now—SLEEP!

Get Grounded and Plug In

{DO THIS TO GET GROUNDED INTO YOUR BODY AND OPEN YOUR MIND TO INTUITIVE THOUGHT. GREAT TO USE IF YOU'RE FEELING SCATTERED, SPACEY, OR PULLED IN TOO MANY DIRECTIONS!}

What you'll need: Five to ten undisturbed minutes. A place to sit quietly.

Stand or sit with your spine straight and your body balanced. Don't cross your legs if you're sitting in a chair or your ankles if you are sitting on the floor. Begin by closing your eyes and becoming aware of the rhythm of your breath—just let it *slow down*. Slowly breathe in through your nose and exhale through your mouth. Imagine all your worries, fears, and mind chatter flowing out of you with each exhalation. Concentrate on your breath and feeling calm and completely present.

In your Mind's Eye, imagine that you have an hourglass figure—if you're lucky, this may only require you to think of your *actual* hourglass figure! Think of the top portion of your body as a wide open funnel, able to let spirit energy in; the narrow middle section of your core as strong and supportive; and the bottom portion of your body as a full skirt sweeping wide around you, grounding you firmly into the Earth. When we get our minds into a balanced state, this is what our *energy body* looks like—open on top, strong in the middle, and grounded to the Earth on bottom.

As you breathe slowly and deeply, visualize yourself as your favorite tree (I like to imagine myself as a strong and mighty oak). Your branches stretch out above, your roots stretch deeply into the ground, and your trunk is straight and strong.

Breathe in through your branches. Imagine the warm sun filling you up. Take the breath right down through your trunk and breathe out strongly through your roots, deep into the ground.

Now breathe in from the Earth, and draw the breath back up through your roots, up through your trunk, and all the way into your branches—out into the fresh air and sun.

Take another breath in through your branches, allowing the sun to fill you up, and again take the breath right down through your trunk and out powerfully through your roots, deep into the Earth.

Now again, breathe in from deep within the Earth, drawing the breath up through your roots, up through your trunk, and all the way into your branches, and out into the sky above. Imagine a current of dynamic white light running through your branches and reaching toward a storm cloud of magnetic light above. Concentrate on this image and continue to breathe, all the while setting the intention to connect with your intuition.

Repeat these two breath sequences for a few minutes.

Once you feel like you've really gotten into the mind-set—after five minutes or fifteen, whatever you need—gradually let the visualization fade and feel yourself deeply rooted into the Earth, centered and grounded in your body, your central column now a clear and open channel for energy to flow into and out of, and your mind wide open and receptive to intuitive clarity.

Let Go and Fill Up

{DO THIS MEDITATION TO RELEASE STRESS AND TOXIC, BLOCKED ENERGY, AND MAKE SPACE FOR POSITIVE THOUGHT.}

What you'll need: Somewhere quiet to lie down.

Start with your simple breathing meditation. After getting as present as possible, locate any tension, stress, negativity, or fear in your body and mind. Continue to breathe and become aware of how you feel and where you feel tension. Can you locate where in your body you are holding on to this negative energy? Is it your head, neck, back, shoulders, stomach, chest? It may be in more than one area. Become mindful of where you are holding stress.

Continue to breathe.

Next, imagine plugs on the soles of your feet. Just as we unplug a bathtub to let the dirty bathwater drain, you're going to unplug the soles of each foot, draining negative, stuck energy from both the left and right sides of your body. Visualize unplugging your feet. Feel a rushing and swirling of energy draining out of each foot. Feel the blocked areas in your body become clear.

Continue to breathe.

Once you feel the draining is complete, visualize lightness within. Concentrate on a white, safe, and loving light filling your body.

Now that you've let go of unwanted negative energy, there's room to bring in fresh, positive, and loving energy. Close your eyes again and go within.

Now imagine an opening at the top of your head and a glass pitcher, or a watering can, filling you up with white light from Source and Spirit. Feel it flood your entire being, from the crown of your head down to the soles of your feet. Imagine the positive light energy washing away all heavy, stuck, dark, negative energy and leaving you feeling light, joyful, and full of optimism.

Come back to this meditation whenever you feel blocked with nasty energy that you want to flush out and release.

White Light Protection (Psychic Shielding)

{DO THIS WHEN YOU WANT TO SHIELD YOURSELF FROM PSYCHIC VAMPIRES AND PROTECT YOUR ENERGY. COME BACK TO IT ANYTIME YOU FEEL DEPLETED OR VULNERABLE.}

What you'll need: Concentration and focus. Other than that, you can do this anywhere and anytime. (I do this meditation every morning before I get out of bed. I hold the vision and set a mental intention to be held in this bubble of safety, light, and love throughout the day. I visualize any toxic energy that I come into contact with as unable to penetrate my bubble.)

Close your eyes and take several deep breaths. Visualize a brilliant white light—brighter than the sun—descending from the crown of your head and slowly expanding all around you, wrapping you in a large bubble of intense, radiant light. As you breathe, the bubble continues to expand in all directions, extending several feet out from your body, shielding your entire body from all negativity and fear-based energy.

Mentally invite your passed loved ones, spirit guides, and Archangel Michael, the angel of protection, into your day, giving them permission to guide and protect you as needed. You might say: *Thank you for fully shielding and protecting me today, in a bubble of white light, from all darkness, negativity, and fear I may encounter. Please bounce all negativity off and away from me. Let my white light transform all darkness back into light and love.*

As you continue to breathe deeply, visualize the light filling your entire being with pure, positive, loving energy. Continue to visualize this protective bubble until you are ready to open your eyes and face the day.

Release the Grief and Forgive

{DO THIS WHEN YOU WANT TO RELEASE PAST HURT AND FRUSTRATION AND RECLAIM YOUR FREEDOM AND PERSONAL POWER.}

What you'll need: A candle and a match. A place to sit quietly.

Find a quiet place to sit quietly. Have your candle and match at your side. Close your eyes and do your simple breathing meditation. Take several deep inhales and exhales and get present. After a few minutes, open your eyes and light your candle while affirming:

> I am letting go of all pain, suffering, and despair I experienced in the past from (this person, situation, my own creation). I surrender it to God's hands and reclaim my freedom and power right now.

Close your eyes once again and mentally invite your spirit guides in to help you release any pain you're holding on to. Imagine your spirit guides taking your icky feelings into the light for healing and transformation.

Breathe. Allow your mind to be still and quiet . . . seeing, hearing, or feeling nothing but the stillness. Just be. Sit in this space of lightness, peace, and love for as long as feels right for you. When you feel ready to let go and release your grief to the Universe, blow out the candle.

Meet Your Guides

{DO THIS MEDITATION WHEN YOU WANT TO MAKE CONTACT WITH YOUR SPIRIT GUIDES.}

What you'll need: Fifteen minutes and a place to sit or lie comfortably.

Start with your simple breathing meditation. Once you feel grounded and connected to the Earth, and your higher self is awakened, imagine yourself in a beautiful setting where you want to meet your spirit guide. Envision a specific spot where you'll meet up each time you want to connect. For me, this is a deck overlooking the ocean with the sun going down. I put myself in this scene and drink in the sights, sounds, and smells of this moment. When I'm in this place, I feel free. Free from the past and free from expectations of the future.

Breathe and meditate on this spot for a few minutes.

Ask mentally or aloud, *"Who are you? How do you work with me? What do you want to teach me? Do you have any messages for me?"* Mentally ask your guide to respond to you and to identify himself or herself with a name or a symbol.

LISTEN!

Pay attention to all your senses. You may get a visual response such as a flash of light. You may hear a whisper or get a strong feeling or knowing. The more you do this, the easier it will become to connect.

When I'm in this meditation, I sit for a minute or two in my comfortable deck chair feeling relaxed and totally present in the moment. Then a combination of deceased relatives, angels, and my guides meet me on the deck. These light beings gather around me in a circle and encourage me to unload. I release my fears, concerns, and anxieties. Once I have emptied out all my frazzled energy, I let their white light of love and truth fill me up. I imagine light coming in through the palms of my outstretched hands and in through my Mind's Eye and inflating me like a white wave. As the light pours in, I receive thoughts, feelings, symbols, and words of guidance. Sometimes it's like watching a movie play out in my mind. Whatever form it takes, I make a conscious effort to stay open and let it all pour in without criticism or self-editing.

When the process is complete (this could be five minutes or an hour later), they slowly pull back their light and disappear and leave me alone in my special place. I come back to the awareness of my body and my breath and feel WIDE AWAKE. I am re-charged and reconnected and even though my spiritual guides are gone for the moment, I don't feel alone. I feel loved, sup-ported, and alive.

Planting the Seeds

{DO THIS WHEN YOU WANT TO CLEAR YOUR MIND OF NEGATIVITY AND MAKE SPACE FOR POSITIVE THOUGHT.}

What you'll need: A quiet place to sit or lie down

Close your eyes, and begin to breathe slowly and deeply. With each breath, let your mind and body relax and let go.

Breathe . . . and allow yourself to drift off into a state of deep relaxation.

Breathe . . . and now imagine a vacuum placed a few inches above the crown of your head, set to a comfortable power, that will allow you to cleanse your mind, body, and spirit of all nega-tive debris. As you breathe, imagine this vacuum sucking up all the stuck and dark energy that no longer serves you.

As you continue to breathe, slowly and deeply, feel your body and mind lightening and softening, as you allow yourself to be cleansed and freed from all that has weighed you down.

And now say aloud:

I free my mind of all unnecessary stress and concerns that only stand in my way.

I am willing to release any worries or cares that weigh me down.

I surrender all resistance and fears that keep me from my highest good.

I say "cancel" to every negative thought that comes into my mind.

I free myself now from all self-destructive thoughts, habits, and behavior

And now, as you continue to breathe, imagine reversing the switch on the vacuum and drawing down a stream of liquid white light into the crown of your head. Allow this bright, powerful, healing light to fill and heal your mind, body, and spirit. Feel it wash away all negative thoughts. Continue to breathe it in, drawing it all the way down into your core and into the soles of your feet. Visualize it expanding out through your physical body and creating a glow on top of your skin. And now say aloud: *I am safe and secure and I only allow positive and loving energy into my life.*

Heart Opener

{DO THIS TO RELEASE ANY NEGATIVITY THAT YOU MAY BE HOLDING IN YOUR HEART.}

What you'll need: A comfy place to sit and a lit candle.

For this meditation, we're going to work with a high spiritual energy known as the violet flame. When we work with the violet flame in meditation, it creates a healing in our body, mind, and soul, stimulating forgiveness and love.

Light your candle, set your gaze upon it, and breathe deeply. Feel it descend into your body from the top of your head, down into your Mind's Eye, through your throat, and into your heart. Continue to breathe deeply and feel the light expand. Let its strength and power engulf you. Mentally call on Spirit, your guides, and your higher self to release you from anything that is blocking your energy. Ask for clarity regarding the source of negativity or fear you may be holding on to. Ask that it reveal itself in either a picture, symbol, word, or feeling. You may also ask to see anyone's face or name that might be hooked into your energy, causing you to feel drained. Continue to breathe and just sit with this for a few minutes, observing what comes up for you. Remind yourself that you are in a safe environment to acknowledge your feelings. Imagine holding your feelings in a big bear hug, or cradling them in your arms. Take three deep breaths and with each exhale, release your feelings back into the flame. Visualize the flame transforming all negative energy into positive, loving, and forgiving energy. Feel the light washing away all feelings of pain, despair, suffering, and resentment. After you've taken three breaths, take one final deep inhale and slowly let it out. Feel the shift in your energy as your heart opens. Now silently give thanks for being in this place of peace, and know that it is always available to you. You can reconnect with it at any time. All you need do is go within.

My Body Is My Temple

{DO THIS WHEN YOU'RE FEELING NEGATIVE TOWARD AND SEPARATE FROM YOUR BODY.}

What you'll need: Five minutes and a quiet place to concentrate.

Start with your simple breathing exercise. Draw your breath and awareness down to the soles of your feet and observe what you're feeling there (tension, aches, tingling).

Mentally thank your feet for carrying you around every day, getting you everywhere you need to go. Send love and gratitude to your feet.

Next, move on up to your ankles, calves, knees. Pay tribute and show gratitude to every major bone and organ you can think of, all the way up to your head. If you get to a part of your body that is prone to injury or often gives you trouble, spend some extra time sending it love and healing energy. (I often say something silly like, *Thank you knees for all that you do. I know I often overlook and sometimes abuse you. I promise to pay more attention to you and treat you sweetly. Don't give up on me!*)

Continue all the way up your body until you feel gratitude for all the work it does for you. Once you feel the process is complete, open up your eyes and get back to the rest of your day.

Appendix B

＊

Additional Meditations for the Hard Core

Just a friendly warning—the following meditations are a bit more advanced and take longer to do.

Energy Clearing and Balancing
Over the Rainbow

Energy Clearing and Balancing

{DO THIS TO KEEP YOUR SPIRITUAL CHANNELS OPEN AND CLEAR. DO A VERSION OF THIS DAILY.}

What you'll need: A quiet space to lie down.

Begin by taking three slow deep breaths, in through your nose and out through your mouth. Continue to breathe slowly and deeply, releasing all tension and stress with each exhale while breathing in positive energy with each inhale. Continue to breathe as you start to shift out of your mind and into your higher self. Notice any fear-based mind thoughts that come in and simply release them to your guides and angels. Just continue to breathe in and out—letting go—and open up to healing, peaceful energy. Once you are relaxed with a quieted mind and feeling a deep sense of inner peace, feel where your body meets the surface of where you're sitting or lying down. Become aware of your body from head to toe, of your weight, of the heaviness of your limbs. Continue to breathe, slowly and deeply. As you do this meditation, imagine climbing a rainbow spiral staircase. Each time you go up and around, imagine lighting up an energy center until you get to the very top.

ROOT CENTER

You'll begin by clearing the energy center at the base of the spine. This is the root chakra. Its energy is red and it grounds us in the physical world, in our natural environment. It's related to our basic needs for survival, security, and safety and when it's balanced, it attracts health, prosperity, and a sense of security into our lives. If this energy center is blocked you may feel fearful, anxious, insecure, and frustrated. Specifically, blockages manifest in an inability to trust nature and in a heightened attention to our material possessions. When our minds are consumed with finances, our careers, and our "stuff," the health of our root center is in trouble. Additionally, when our root center is out of whack, physical problems like obesity, anorexia nervosa, and knee troubles can occur. Root body parts include the hips, legs, lower back, and sexual organs.

In your Mind's Eye, visualize this particular energy center; note its color and vitality. As you meditate, take note of any symbolic symptoms of disease. Have you been caring well for you body lately? Does your root energy appears dusty, dirty, torn, or a brownish-red color? Imagine your hands or those of your guardian angel massaging your root energy center. Clean away any and all dirt and darkness, and dump it into an imaginary bucket placed before you. Allow those hands to repair any imperfections, and when you feel that your root center is cleaned, hand the bucket to your angel and watch as she flies away carrying the bucket off into healing light. Turn your attention back to your root energy center. It is clean and illuminated. See it as a translucent ruby red, like stained glass appears when sunlight passes through it. Imagine the room glowing red with this energy and feel its strength and power. See red swirls of energy flowing through your root center. As the energy swirls, visualize your root center growing large and strong. Allow the energy to fill your root center until it extends several feet out from your body in all directions. Visualize and feel your root center as a brilliant red swirling vortex of physical energy.

Breathe.

SACRAL CENTER

Next, move your focus up to the area between your navel and the base of your spine. This is your sacral, or belly chakra. It governs your sense of self-worth, your confidence in your own creativity, and your ability to relate to others in an open and friendly way. It's influenced by how emotions were expressed or repressed in the family during childhood. This energy center is orange. When this energy center is in balance, or flowing freely, we're sexually fulfilled and we have the ability to accept change. Blockage manifests as emotional problems or sexual guilt. We may feel emotionally explosive or manipulative, be obsessed with thoughts of sex, or have a lack of energy. Physical problems may include kidney weakness, stiff lower back, constipation, and muscle spasms. Take a moment to observe it and note its color and vitality. Our thoughts and feelings regarding cravings, addictions, and our body image affect the sacral center. If you're holding on to any stress or concerns about your body, your sacral center will appear small and dirty. And you may feel sluggish, insecure, or have difficulty in expressing your feelings.

As you breathe deeply into the sacral center, ask those invisible hands to cleanse this area, to repair or heal it. Now simply toss all darkness and fear into the bucket and send it off with your angel to transform the energy back into light. Visualize the sacral center again. It is now clean and balanced, glowing a bright orange like a fresh tangerine.

Set the intentions to draw in orange creative energy and feel the space around you begin to radiate orange. Feel the energy swirl into your sacrum, charging it with vitality, with creativity and clear thought. Watch as your sacral center grows and whirls, until it extends several feet out from your body.

Continue to breathe.

THE CENTER OF THE SOLAR PLEXUS

Now turn your attention to the solar plexus, located right behind the navel. This chakra spins at a faster rate than the root and sacral centers. It appears in shades of bright yellow. This energy center relates to power, will, emotions, and ego. It gives us a sense of personal power in the world. When healthy, this chakra brings us energy and effectiveness. Blockage manifests as anger or a sense of victimization, a need to dominate, insecurity, and distrust in the natural flow. Physical problems may include digestive difficulties, liver problems, diabetes, nervous exhaustion, and food allergies.

Take a few moments to examine this energy center and note its color and appearance. Mentally ask yourself, *Do I have fear of owning my power? Have I had any experiences lately in which I've felt overpowered by another person? Do I have any fears of being controlled by others? Or a fear of losing control?*

When we hold on to these types of fears, the solar plexus will take on a muddy yellow color and appear quite small. Now allow the invisible hands of your higher self or your angel to cleanse this center and heal it, discarding any impurities or imperfections into the bucket. Then send the bucket into the loving hands of your angel for purification and healing. Now return your attention to the solar plexus. It is now a clean, bright yellow, and perfectly enlarged. Mentally ask Source to send you yellow energy to achieve your goals and to be of service in the highest way. Feel the yellow energy surrounding your body. And with a tingle, feel the energy swirl into your solar plexus. In your Mind's Eye, see your root center, glowing and whirling, your sacral center pulsing brilliantly, and your solar plexus glowing brightly and extending several feet out from your body.

Continue to breathe.

HEART CENTER

Now breathe yourself into the middle of your chest, to the heart center. The fourth chakra is known as the seat of the soul and it connects our mind, body, and spirit. It glows a beautiful shade of green and it is the center of love, compassion, and spirituality. This center dictates our ability to give and receive love, show compassion, be empathetic, and see the good in people. Blockage can manifest as immune system or heart problems, or a lack of compassion. When the heart center is out of balance you may feel sorry for yourself, paranoid, indecisive, afraid of letting go, afraid of getting hurt, or unworthy of love. The heart center marks the beginning of the upper chakras, which govern spiritual issues, versus the lower chakras, which govern physical and material issues.

Take a moment and examine this energy center. Note its color and vitality. If you notice any darkness in or around your heart, gently invite those invisible hands to cleanse and purify it. As you breathe deeply into your heart center, reflect on how you've been feeling emotionally lately. Ask yourself, *Am I holding on to any anger, resentment, or sadness? Have I experienced any challenges with regard to giving or receiving love?* If so, it's now safe to release any fears, imperfections, or impurities into the bucket, and send them off with your angel into the light where they are fully healed. As you continue to breathe deeply, focus your attention back on the heart center. It is clean and a beautiful green color. It whirls strongly and brightly. Mentally ask Spirit and Source to open your heart fully to the world and to everyone who crosses your path. Ask that your heart be filled with loving energy so that you may be an expression of love, unconditionally giving and receiving love in every moment. Feel the green energy whirling into your heart. Watch your heart expand and glow and spin with this new energy.

Continue to breathe.

THROAT CENTER

Now breathe yourself into your throat center, where your throat chakra is located. It is a sky blue and spins at a faster rate. It governs communication and speaking your truth. When unbalanced, you may feel timid, want to hold back, and feel unable to express your thoughts. Physical illnesses or ailments include hyperthyroid, skin irritations, ear infections, sore throat, inflammations, laryngitis, and back pain. When this chakra is balanced we may feel inspired musically or artistically, and have the ability to speak and write effectively. Examine this energy center, noting its color and any imperfections. And now mentally ask yourself, *Have I been honoring my own beliefs and speaking my truth when I should? Have I been talking over others or not listening well lately? Have I been feeling shy and afraid to extend my energy in communication with others? Have I been feeling choked up lately, having a difficult time expressing my feelings and emotions?* If you are holding on to any fears, your throat center may appear a cloudy bluish-gray color. Allow those angelic hands to cleanse and purify this energy center.

When you're finished, once again, send the impurities into the bucket, into your angel's loving hands and off to the light. Now your energy is clean, strong, and a bright blue. Feel the air fill with blue universal energy. Feel the throat open as this energy swirls into the throat center. This energy is magnetic, drawing others to you.

Continue to breathe.

MIND'S EYE CENTER

Now breathe yourself up to the area between your two eyes in the brow area, the Mind's Eye, which is the pineal gland. This energy center has the capability of looking upward, where we see clairvoyantly. Your Mind's Eye center is a deep indigo blue color with sparkles of purple and white light. It governs psychic vision and intuition. Blockage manifests as a closed third eye, blindness to psychic visions, bad retention of dreams, the rejection of spiritual aspects, and a focus on science and intellect only. Physical symptoms may include headaches, blurred vision, blindness, and eyestrain. When this chakra is balanced and open it allows us to see clearly, in all directions of time, and we may experience telepathy, astral travel, and past lives. We lose any and all fear of death; we are not attached to material things.

As you visualize this oval-shaped eye, you may feel a slight pressure in this area. Examine this center and note the color and any imperfections. Perhaps it's closed due to fear of a past traumatic experience or the fear of not knowing the future. Perhaps it's no longer spinning out of neglect. If you sense your third eye is partially or fully closed, allow the angelic hands to cleanse it, to remove and heal any blocks and release them into the bucket and into your angel's hands and into the light.

Now visualize your third eye center. You may notice an eye staring back at you, beautiful, bright, and indigo. Know that infinite psychic energy is available to you. Now is a good time to offer a prayer for increased psychic power and insight.

CROWN CENTER

Now breathe yourself all the way up to the crown of your head. This is your crown center and it should appear as a violet color, fading into a bright white halo above your head. Your crown center connects you with Spirit, Source, and messages from higher realms. It is your connection to a timeless, spaceless place of oneness and all knowing, enlightenment, and spirituality. Blockage of the crown manifests as feelings of separation and loneliness. You may feel depressed, unsatisfied, and joyless and feel an inability to overcome anxiety and fear. Illnesses may include migraine headaches and depression. When in a balanced state, this energy center provides us knowledge, wisdom, understanding, spiritual connection, and bliss. It allows us total access to the unconscious and subconscious minds. An open crown can feel like a floating or tingling sensation on the top of the head. As you examine this energy center, take pause and reflect on your spirituality. Mentally ask yourself, *Have I been open to divine guidance and insights? Have I taken the time to slow down and still my mind through meditation? Do I listen to and trust my inner voice of wisdom?*

Note any blocks within or around your crown center and allow any healing needed to take place. Simply allow the divine hands to cleanse and heal, and release all blocks created from fear that would leave you feeling separated and alone. See your angel carrying away these impurities in the bucket and off into the divine healing light. Now see your crown center as brilliant, violet, and glowing white around the outside. Mentally reach out to your divine source, to God or the Universe. Feel loving energy flowing back to and through you. Offer gratitude for your spiritual connection. Feel the violet energy flowing in, embracing your spirit with love. Visualize your crown growing larger and larger with white energy that surrounds your whole body.

All your energy centers are now clean, charged, and perfectly balanced. Visualize the clean and clear line of spiritual energy beginning at your root center, up through the sacrum, into the solar plexus, up to the heart center, into the throat and third eye centers, and finally into your crown. Your energy is now full of vitality, spinning and glowing brightly. You are completely replenished, calm, and peaceful. Your intuitive and spiritual channels are now open and activated.

Your energy is now flowing like a river of light though your seven centers, and you want to keep it that way. With your energy channels wide open, you become extra sensitive to intuitive and outside energy.

Over the Rainbow

{DO THIS MEDITATION WHEN YOU WANT TO MAKE CONTACT WITH YOUR SPIRIT GUIDES.}

What you'll need: Fifteen minutes and a place to sit or lie comfortably.

Take a long deep breath, close your eyes, and begin to relax. Set the intention to relax every muscle in your body from the top of your head to the tips of your toes.

As you inhale and exhale, notice your breathing; notice the rhythm of it for a moment. Be aware of any sounds around you; whatever you hear from now on will only serve to relax you. And as you exhale, release any tension and stress you may be holding on to. As you inhale, imagine a cleansing white light washing away any stressful thoughts in your mind; begin to feel them melt away, allowing for a deep sense of inner peace and relaxation.

Begin to feel all tension melting away from your body, starting with the muscles in your face. Let your jaw relax and release all tension in your temples and forehead. As you feel them relax, you'll be able to drift and float into a deeper and deeper level of total relaxation. Rest your eyes and imagine your eyelids feeling so heavy, so comfortable, so relaxed. And now let the muscles in the back of your neck and shoulders relax. Feel a heavy weight being lifted off your shoulders, as you feel relieved, lighter and more relaxed. And feel that soothing relaxation go down your back, down, down, down, to the lower part of your back, and those muscles let go, and with every breath you inhale, just feel your body drifting, floating, down deeper, down deeper, down deeper into total relaxation. Let all of the muscles in your shoulders, running down your arms to your fingertips, relax. And let your arms feel so heavy and so comfortable, so relaxed. And now inhale once again and relax your chest muscles. As you exhale, feel your stomach muscles relax. Let them go and let all of the muscles in your legs relax, completely relax right to the tips of your toes. Notice how very comfortable your body feels, just drifting and floating, deeper, deeper, deeper. And as you are relaxing deeper and deeper, imagine a beautiful rainbow bridge. This bridge is a few feet in the distance, and as you make your way closer to the rainbow bridge, each gentle step takes you closer to the safe, beautiful, and special place that lies on the other side of this bridge.

Breathe.

And now you are standing at the base of the rainbow bridge. You feel a complete sense of freedom and weightlessness. You feel no fear. You feel absolute trust, protection, and security. You're reminded of your soul's knowing that you are filled and surrounded by the universal light and love of Source.

Breathe.

As you take your first step onto the brilliant rainbow bridge, you feel an overwhelming sense of peace and calm flow through you. You are totally immersed and surrounded by the first color, red. Breathe in this deep ruby red and feel yourself taking on all the positive aspects of this color.

Breathe.

Now feel yourself gliding out of the red color and into the next color of the rainbow bridge, the color orange. Again, feel or imagine yourself pausing here in the orange energy. Breathe in this beautiful shade of orange. Next, find yourself moving into the next color, yellow. Pause and allow this bright yellow light to fill your entire being. As you feel lighter and freer, you drift into the middle of the bridge and the next color, emerald green. Take a deep breath and fill yourself with the healing energies of this green light. Once you're ready, feel yourself gently floating into the next color, sky blue. Breathe it in completely and allow this brilliant shade of blue to fill you with a sense of deep peace and calm. Now continue moving forward along the bridge, into the next color, indigo—a dark purplish-blue. Allow this deep color to fill and surround your body and open up your third eye. Now glide into the next color, which is violet. Feel or imagine that this powerful violet color is absorbed into every level of your being. This violet light serves as protection from all lower energies, while lifting you higher and deeper into relaxation and love. As you glide toward the end of the bridge and into the last color, radiant white light, you feel a deep sense of well-being and positive energy flow through you. Pause for a moment while you soak up the rejuvenating and healing white light. As you move off the bridge and onto the other side, you emerge deeper into this beautiful white light, feeling a sense of oneness with Spirit.

Breathe.

You pause for a moment as you sense a gentle presence standing at your side. You are filled with feelings of unconditional love and acceptance and realize the presence is that of your spirit guides and guardian angel. Take a moment to allow these angelic beings to reveal themselves to you. It may or may not be energy you know in this lifetime. Mentally ask your guides and angel their names. Pause.

Now ask your spirit guides and angel for any messages that would be in your highest good in this moment. Your spirits' response may come in the form of a vision in your Mind's Eye, a word, phrase, or dialogue in your inner voice, or an impression of thoughts and feelings in your mind and body. Just breathe deeply, relax, and allow the energy and angelic information to flow to and through you, knowing you are safe, protected, and deeply loved.

Pause for a few minutes.

Once you feel complete, healed, and at peace with the guidance and loving presence of your angels and guides, gently move forward into the bright white light . . . feeling a deeper and deeper connection and oneness with Spirit and Source. As you drift into the light, you start to notice a meadow with a gentle flowing brook in the distance. You slowly move forward, feeling drawn toward this healing and peaceful energy. As you approach the grassy meadow, you notice a bench facing the water, and somebody sitting on it. You approach the bench and feel a deep loving presence inviting you in. You feel inspired to sit down next to this familiar soul presence and immediately recognize it as a deceased loved one. You are overwhelmed with emotion as you reconnect with this spirit. Now spend some time

in this space with your loved one. Allow in any other spirit energies important to you, keeping the intention for only those in
your highest and best good to come forth. Bask in this loving
and light energy for however long feels perfect for you.

Breathe.

You are now ready to make your way back to the rainbow
bridge. As you leave the special bench by the brook, you are filled
with a deep sense of inner peace and well-being. You know these
positive feelings will stay with you long after this experience is
over, for the rest of this day and evening and into the days to
come. Allow these positive feelings to grow stronger and stronger, and know that each time you choose to do this meditation,
you'll be able to relax more deeply and gain greater clarity and
truth. Regardless of the stress and tension in your life, you may
now feel more at peace, more calm, more relaxed with the knowing you can always reconnect with your spirit guides and loved
ones in Spirit. All you need to do is open your mind and heart
to receive their loving energy.

Breathe.

You float back toward the base of the bridge and gently step from
the white light into the violet color and on into the indigo, gliding next into the sky blue, and now halfway across the bridge
into the emerald green . . . gently drifting into the sunny yellow . . . and on into the orange and, finally, the ruby red color.
As you step off the rainbow bridge, you feel a sense of gratitude
for your experience with your loved ones and guides in Spirit.

ACKNOWLEDGMENTS

I wish to express my heartfelt appreciation to those who have supported and assisted me along this journey and in making *Spirited* a reality.

First and foremost, to my cowriter, Samantha Rose, "thank you" doesn't seem to do justice to her collaboration on this book. Her guidance, assistance, and belief in me have been major contributions to the quality and integrity of the material presented here. Samantha's ability to fashion my thoughts and experiences into an engaging narrative has made it possible for me to share my story and my understanding of this work. I am grateful for her skeptical, yet open, mind and heart, her sensitivity, and her masterful writing.

My deepest gratitude goes to my literary agent, Yfat Reiss Gendell, for following her own intuition in seeking me out to create this book. I am still in awe of the divine synchronicity of how our paths crossed. She has demonstrated unwavering support and creative brilliance since the very first phone conversation. It has been a privilege and honor to work with Yfat and the Foundry team, especially Stéphanie Abou, whose relentless pursuit and hard work in getting this book into the foreign markets has proven to be incredibly successful.

I owe a great debt of gratitude to my amazing editor, Sally Kim, and all the wonderful people at HarperCollins, whose talents, energy, and support have made my dream a reality. The day I first stepped foot in HarperCollins, I knew I had found my home. I am grateful for their

dedication to this book, appreciation of the work, valuable editorial sug-
gestions, unending patience, and encouragement.

The ride wouldn't be as fun without my business partner, Rick Bar-
lowe, and the Sheridan Taylor group. He has been the driving force behind many projects, this book included. From the day we met, he has
taken me under his wing, treating me and my family like his own. I am
very grateful for his generosity, kindness, and most of all his assistance
in getting my work out to those in need.

I am eternally grateful for my beloved, Brian: my husband, my
manager, my everything! He has allowed me to grow and soar, while at
the same time keeping me grounded in this world. He is the reason why
I've been able to serve so many, as he has taken care of all the earthly
details, which has allowed me to focus on my spiritual work. His unconditional love, support, and belief in me has brought me to this
"now moment." I thank him from the bottom of my heart and soul.
I LOVE YOU!

My heart swells with gratitude when it comes to my two Earth angels, Jakob and Sam. I thank God each day that they chose me to be
their "Earth mommy." Every day they serve as my teachers, and I'm
grateful for the joy, love, and magic they bring to my life.

My mom, who has become one of my biggest fans and greatest sup-
porters. I have her to thank for my solid work ethic, as she has served as
an example and inspiration for me to show up each day and make the
world a better place. I am grateful for her unconditional love and belief
in me!

My brothers, Zach and Baruch, and my sister-in-law, Ariela, whose
support of the path I have chosen and belief in me has made all the difference. I have my older brother, Baruch, to thank for starting me on
this journey. He bought me my first spiritual books and journals when I
was in high school, the very first of which was inscribed with "never
forget that you are not alone and there is something beyond yourself, an
energy, God, from which you can draw strength. Create and live with

passion." His example of *walking the walk* continues to serve as my inspiration to do the same.

And my love and thanks go out to the rest of my extended family, for supporting me over the years as I've journeyed down this unconventional path. I am humbled and amazed to see the transformations in many of my family members, as they've opened their minds and embraced my work.

My deepest thanks to all the people who shared their stories in this book. It is my hope that through their experiences, others will be touched, comforted, and inspired.

A very special thank you to James Van Praagh for so graciously writing the foreword to this book. He has served as one of my great teachers along this path, offering his support and wisdom on many levels. It has been an honor to work with him in the past, and I'm grateful to now join him in opening people's minds and hearts to this healing work.

Words fail to express how incredibly grateful I am to my loyal clientele for allowing me the opportunity to do God's work every day.

There are countless additional people who have touched my life over the years, in profound and meaningful ways. I extend a big thank you to all of these special souls who have helped to shape my life and this book: my teachers, spiritual companions, and beloved friends, who have shared their wisdom, love, and acceptance of who I am.

And finally, simple words don't do justice when it comes to acknowledging the eternal presence, guidance, love, support, and wisdom of my spiritual guides, Master Crew and M3. I am grateful for their daily reminder to "just be me" and to simply "just be."